The Christian Way

A GUIDE TO THE CHRISTIAN LIFE BASED ON THE SERMON ON THE MOUNT

By

John W. Miller

HERALD PRESS
Scottdale, Pennsylvania
Kitchener, Ontario

Credit: At a number of places in this book short quotations are used from *The New English Bible*. These are used by permission. © The Delegates of the Oxford University Press and the Syndics of the Cambridge University Press, 1961. The additional Scripture quotations are from the Revised Standard Version of the Bible, copyrighted 1946 and 1952 by National Council of Churches. Used by permission.

Preface

As most people now realize, these are critical days for the Christian churches. Old, established structures of authority and equally well established doctrinal traditions are coming apart, and it is not yet clear what will replace them. Such times of crisis drive us back to the ultimate source of our faith, Jesus Himself, and to the one place where we have a record of His life, death, and resurrection, the Gospels.

Among the treasured documents of the church to be found in the Gospels are three chapters of quotations from the teaching ministry of Jesus, Matthew 5-7. These chapters are traditionally referred to as the "Sermon on the Mount." This of course is a misnomer, for the materials here are far from sermonic in style. They consist rather of highly condensed, powerfully concentrated sayings of Jesus on a wide variety of subjects. The Sermon on the Mount is the most extensive single collection of Jesus' teachings available today.

This being so it might be expected that this document would have played a major role in church history as a source of recurrent, creative, and authoritative instruction.

Surprisingly, however, such has not been the case. As it turned out, the church during the second to the fifth centuries became engrossed with a set of dogmas and creeds of its own making and these came to occupy the crucial place in the thinking of the church accorded in the beginning to the life and teachings of Jesus. Acts 2:42. Efforts were made throughout Christian history to correct this imbalance, but in the larger communions of Christendom these historic creeds continue to function in an all too decisive way in defining what the Christian faith is all about. As a result Jesus Himself is deprived of any significant authority in the church as a spokesman for His own movement.

A new day may be dawning, however, with the emergence in recent times of biblical studies that point ever more strongly to the importance of the synoptic Gospels (Matthew, Mark, and Luke) for the life and growth of early Christianity.* A most striking example of this development is the growing appreciation among New Testament scholars of the Sermon on the Mount itself. Scholarship now recognizes in this unique collection of Jesus' words a prime example of early Christian catechism.** "Catechism" refers to instruction given to converts at the point of their en-

---

*See bibliography in the appendix. Also Donald T. Rowlingson, "The Jesus of History and Christian Faith," *The Christian Century*, Dec. 25, 1968, pp. 1619 to 1621.
**See especially Joachim Jeremias, *The Sermon on the Mount*, Fortress Press, 1963.

trance into the Christian church. Far then from the marginal set of teachings they have become in contemporary Christianity, these words of Jesus in the Sermon on the Mount were regarded by the early church as of decisive importance for every newly converted Christian. It was on teachings of this kind that the Christian church at the time of its origin drew inspiration for its provocative and winsome life style.

I first became aware of this evaluation of the Sermon on the Mount at a time when I myself had become responsible for teaching a group of Christian converts. As I considered what materials I might use for their instruction, I began to realize that such occasions are critical moments not only for those seeking instruction but also for the instructors. Catechism requires that we select from the multitude of ideas and traditions that have come to be associated with Christianity those which are of first importance—truly an overwhelming task! Small wonder then that on such occasions we look to higher authority. But which higher authority? Church history is strewn with catechisms and instruction manuals, many of them conflicting, most of them antiquated.

The biblical studies referred to above provided a most welcome answer to our quest. If the early church instructed its converts on the basis of the Sermon on the Mount, why could not the same be done today? And in any case, is it not reasonable, yes obvious that the initial training of those who confess Jesus as Messianic Lord should be guided by just such a collection of His most important words?

The following manual reflects, in part at least, our subsequent experience in using the Sermon on the Mount in instructional work with candidates for church membership. The manual itself of course has no other purpose than to serve the Gospel text. At the same time it should be kept in mind that it is not a commentary, strictly speaking. It focuses not so much on the meaning of the text for its original audience as on its significance for our lives today.

It goes without saying that a number of people have had a part in the preparation of this manual. I should like to record my gratitude first of all to Gerald Studer, Clarence Jordan, John Howard Yoder, Harry Spaeth, Virgil Vogt, Alan and Jeanne Howe, and Julius Belser, who read it in its early stages of development and gave it the benefit of their criticism and encouragement. Dr. Otto Klassen reviewed my comments on Jesus' teaching about sexual life and offered several helpful suggestions, which I have tried to incorporate into my discussion.

The manual is being published at this time as a result of the initiative of the Counsel and Reference Committee of the Mennonite churches under the leadership of Paul Lederach. This committee's interest in encouraging the use of the Sermon on the

Mount as a catechism among Mennonites is heartening, suggesting that this may be an idea whose time has come.

Finally I want to thank my wife, as well as our fellow members in the Reba Place Fellowship, for sharing in the study of this Sermon on many occasions, but most of all for their comradeship in trying to live it.

Table of Contents

	Preface	3
I.	The Sermon in Summary	11
II.	Introduction (Matthew 5:1, 2)	14
III.	Self-Examination (Matthew 5:3-16)	22
IV.	Our Life with Others (Matthew 5:17-48)	39
V.	Our Life with God (Matthew 6)	66
	Concluding Admonitions and Warnings (Matthew 7)	92

Appendixes

1. Questions for Self-examination	122
2. A Covenant for Christian Disciples:	124
a. Concerning Our Life with Others	124
b. Concerning Our Life with God	125
c. Concerning Our Practice of Discipleship	126
3. "Be Careful!" An Admonition	127
4. "This Is How You Should Pray"	128
5. Property Attitudes Checklist	130
6. Four Concluding Admonitions	132
7. Four Closing Warnings	134
Bibliographical Comments	136

"Everyone who hears these words of mine
and does them
will be like a wise man
who built his house upon a rock. . . .

"Everyone who hears these words of mine
and does not do them
will be like a foolish man
who built his house upon the sand."

Jesus (Matthew 7:24, 26)

I

The Sermon in Summary

The teachings of Jesus in the Sermon on the
Mount are carefully arranged. They deal in
sequence with the major spheres of life: our
personal life, our life with others, our relation
to God, and the various problems confronting
us as we seek to act upon these teachings in
our daily life. Prior to taking up a study of
the various smaller units of the Sermon scan
Matthew 5 to 7 and notice the general organi-
zation and content of the Sermon as a whole.
The following summaries are provided as a
guide for this preliminary survey.

Introduction (Matthew 5:1, 2)

The editorial introduction to the Sermon in
Matthew 5:1, 2 links the teachings of Jesus
here to the life of Jesus as described in
Matthew 4. This suggests the importance
of understanding the teachings of Jesus in the
context of His life, and especially in the setting
of His Messianic mission as described in that
chapter.

Self-Examination (Matthew 5:3-16)

The Sermon opens with a series of startling declarations frequently referred to as Beatitudes. In these Beatitudes certain persons are singled out: the poor in spirit, the mourners, the meek, those who hunger for righteousness, the merciful, the pure in heart, the peacemakers, those who suffer as a consequence of doing right. These are declared blessed because of the great destiny toward which they are moving. This part of the Sermon awakens within us an awareness of those qualities that should mark the lives of "kingdom" citizens and calls for self-examination.

Our Life with Others (Matthew 5:17-48)

In the second major section of the Sermon the declarative style of teaching gives way to an imperative style and the focus on ourselves is exchanged for a focus on life with others. Jesus identifies some of the destructive forces at work in human relations: anger, lust, falsehood, retaliation, and hatred of enemies. He calls His disciples to "fulfill" Israel's legal and prophetic heritage ("the law and the prophets") by becoming a community of peace, purity, integrity, and love.

Our Life with God (Matthew 6)

In the third major section of the Sermon the imperative style of teaching continues but the subject matter changes. These paragraphs concentrate on our relation to God.

12

Three spheres of life vital to this relationship are discussed: piety, prayer, and property. In dealing with these Jesus uncovers two major problems: hypocrisy and anxiety. He calls for a sincere trust toward God as the antidote both to the hypocrisy that corrupts the piety of the religious and the anxiety that mars the prayers and practical affairs of the "Gentiles."

Concluding Admonitions and Warnings (Matthew 7)

In the fourth and last section of the Sermon it is as if the question were being asked, "How shall we live up to the Sermon's high challenge in the midst of the problems, the weaknesses, the uncertainties, the evil, and the confusion within us and around us?" Four admonitions and four warnings alert us to the most critical problems confronting the Christian movement as it seeks to fulfill its calling and mission in the world.

II

Introduction

(Matthew 5:1, 2)

"Seeing the crowds, he went up on the mountain, and when he sat down his disciples came to him. And he opened his mouth and taught them" (Matthew 5:1, 2).

These few words introducing the Sermon on the Mount relate it to the events in the life of Jesus just preceding it. The Sermon on the Mount has come down to us, not as an independent booklet, but as a part of Matthew's Gospel. It is anchored in the life of Jesus. If we ignore this fact and too quickly transplant the Sermon on the Mount to our own situation, whatever it might be, we may miss or distort its message. Our first task, then, in studying the Sermon on the Mount is to gain as clear an understanding as we can of its setting in the life of Jesus.

A striking feature of Jesus' life at the time He withdrew to teach the Sermon on the Mount was the enormous crowd of people that pressed upon Him wherever He appeared. "So his fame spread throughout all Syria"

(4:24) . . . "and great crowds followed him from Galilee and the Decapolis and Jerusalem and Judea and from beyond the Jordan" (4:25). It was upon "seeing" these crowds that Jesus "went up on the mountain" and began instructing His disciples (5:1). Clearly Matthew's Gospel wants us to understand that it was the presence of these crowds that prompted Jesus to withdraw and teach the Sermon on the Mount.

This being the case it is important that we ask: Who were these crowds? Why did they flock to Jesus? What were they seeking and what was His response?

The answer to these questions can be found by reading Matthew 4, a chapter that functions in many respects as a portal to the Sermon on the Mount. Four events in the life of Jesus stand out in the narrative there:

1. Jesus' rejection of popular Messianic expectations (4:1-11).

2. His call for change in anticipation of the kingdom of God (4:17).

3. The formation of a disciple community (4:18-22).

4. His ministry to the sick (4:23-25).

To understand the setting of the Sermon on the Mount and the significance of the crowds pressing upon Jesus at this moment of His life we must be clear about the meaning of these four actions.

1. *Jesus' Rejection of Popular Messianic Expectations*

The Israel of Jesus' day was a conquered

and humiliated people not unlike the many colonial or semi-colonial societies of our own time. Roman soldiers tramped her countryside; Roman overlords bled her economy.

The response of the Israelite masses to these dire circumstances was as varied as that among oppressed peoples today. Some Israelites collaborated with the foreign rulers. Others despaired of doing anything and tried to make the best of a bad situation. And still others secretly fostered rebellion. Guerrilla forces mobilized behind the scenes and stirred the hopes of the people in the direction of violent overthrow of the occupation forces. Messianic expectations blended with these hopes. The Messiah looked for in these circles was a warrior figure who would lead the armies of Israel to victory. From this triumphant act would flow economic prosperity and the restoration of religious vitality.

The temptations which assailed Jesus following His baptism must be seen against the background of these widespread hopes and expectations. He saw and felt the people's desperate economic need. He witnessed their longing for renewed faith in God. He experienced within Himself their hunger for freedom. And in the face of these needs He was tempted by the possibility of a Messianic strategy that, had He taken it, might have joined His name to that of guerrilla leaders of an earlier generation.

But He did not take that way. The main point of the temptation narrative is to tell

16

us that He rejected the thought of becoming an economic "bread" Messiah (4:3). He turned away from the role of a wonder-working faith revivalist (4:5, 6). And He spurned the offer of political power and glory (4:8, 9). The first He saw would not answer the deeper needs of men ("Man shall not live by bread alone"). The second He rejected as out of harmony with the character of God ("You shall not tempt the Lord your God"). And the third He believed would lead away from loyalty to God into satanic compromise and pride ("You shall worship the Lord your God and him only shall you serve").

The charge brought against Jesus at the time of His crucifixion was that He sought to be king of the Jews. In the eyes of Rome He was only another in a long line of political troublemakers. The temptation narratives, however, make it clear that Rome was wrong. Jesus rejected the way of violent revolution, not, however, without a struggle. That in itself is significant. It suggests how deeply He felt the need for change.

2. *His Call for Change in Anticipation of the Kingdom of God*

Instead of launching a military crusade against Rome, Jesus began to preach, saying, "Repent, for the kingdom of heaven is at hand" (Matthew 4:17).

"And he went about all Galilee, teaching in their synagogues and preaching the gospel of the kingdom" (4:23).

This itinerant preaching and teaching mission marks the opening phase of the public life of Jesus. It singles the launching of *His* movement. The few terse sentences that describe it leave us with many questions. Nevertheless, this much is clear:

a. He called for change. The word "repent" has been much softened by use through the ages. On the lips of Jesus it was a mandate for radical change. Like the radicals of His time and ours, He was not content with the status quo.

b. The changes called for were directed toward the formation of a new society. Jesus heralded the coming of a "kingdom." To the ears of His contemporaries, longing as they were for a politically free Israel, this could mean only one thing. The time of the long-hoped-for liberation from Rome and all foreign oppression had arrived.

c. But a third fact is decisive: The kingdom announced by Jesus was the "kingdom of heaven," or the "kingdom of God," as the other Gospels term it. The word "God" or "heaven" took the proclamation out of the sphere of ordinary human affairs. It linked the message of Jesus with Israel's prophetic expectations of a society to be governed directly by God. "My kingdom is not of this world," Jesus was to say later on in His life. And yet His kingdom was to touch and shape the life of this world as no human power could.

But what more precisely does all this mean?

3. *The Formation of the Disciple Community*

As if to answer this question Jesus began calling disciples. "Follow me!" He said to one man after another. In the context of His announcement of the kingdom of God, this act had enormous significance. It marked the beginning of the formation of the society He was proclaiming.

In calling disciples Jesus moved from theory to practice, from talk to action, from promise to realization. In this act He consciously established Himself as the Teacher-Leader of an identifiable movement. He gathered a group of men to Himself, promised to train them in the life of the kingdom and in turn use them to advance His cause ("Follow me, and I will make you fishers of men"). These disciples He bound to Himself with ties stronger than blood ("He who loves father or mother more than me is not worthy of me," Matthew 10:37), yes, stronger than life itself ("He who does not take his cross and follow me is not worthy of me. He who finds his life will lose it, and he who loses his life for my sake will find it," Matthew 10:38, 39). Many who heard Him recognized the authority behind His summons. They left everything and followed Him. Now they were His men, ready to train for His movement.

4. *His Ministry of Healing*

Instead, however, of hiding out with His men in the hills, as might be expected of a radical leader, Jesus moved freely among the people, and instead of training His disciples in the arts of war, He began a ministry of compassionate healing. "And they brought him all the sick, those afflicted with various diseases and pains, demoniacs, epileptics, and paralytics, and he healed them" (4:24). The effect of this healing ministry upon the people of Palestine is not difficult to imagine. Something new was taking place. A man who preached radical change was healing! A man who spoke of a revolutionary kingdom was casting out demons! A man who proclaimed the reality of God was performing acts of mercy unheard of in their scope and effectiveness! Small wonder that the crowds streamed to Him from far and wide.

Was this the long-awaited Messiah? the great Deliverer spoken of by the prophets?

We have come to the point where we can begin to sense something of the setting of the Sermon on the Mount. Jesus had launched a movement. The watchword of that movement was "change." Its goal was a new political order, the kingdom of God. Its most visible sign was healing. Already a few men had broken with family and jobs and organized themselves around Jesus. When He withdrew to the "mountain," it was these men, *disciples*, who came to Him. They were like soldiers coming to their general, like guerrillas coming to their leader. They were staking their lives on Him. He must show them the way, the strategy by which the movement would succeed. They were waiting to hear about the kingdom of God and what it would mean for them to be its citizens and share in its triumph.

The Sermon on the Mount is Jesus' response. In it He describes the citizens of this new order, suggests the quality of their personal, social, and spiritual life, and indicates the strategy by which they will win their way in the world.

You who take up this study, having enlisted in this movement in our time, should pause at this point to reflect on your readiness. Perhaps in considering Christianity you had in mind simply joining a "church." You may not have thought of the church as a "movement" calling for radical changes in your life. Or you may have thought that Christianity was primarily a matter of believing certain dogmas. You did not realize that it is far more a call to action, a call to discipleship and sometimes hard obedience. Perhaps you thought that your main responsibility as a Christian would be to go to worship services on Sunday and live a respectable life. You did not realize that joining up would involve you in a whole new life style, one that might well bring you into opposition to the "kingdoms of this world." Consider: Do you want to leave the crowd and join the disciples who follow Jesus in this radical way?

III

Self-Examination

(Matthew 5:3-16)

A. Introduction

The Sermon on the Mount opens with a series of highly charged statements, often referred to as the Beatitudes. In these Beatitudes Jesus identifies a certain group of people and calls them blessed because of the great destiny toward which they are moving.

The style of teaching here is typical of Jewish instruction. An example can be found in Psalm 1 of the Old Testament Book of Psalms. There is nothing, however, in the literature of Israel to compare with the psychological scope, the personal intensity, or the prophetic certainty of the Beatitudes. In the Beatitudes Jesus shares with us His own passionate vision of man as he might be were he to realize his innermost calling and destiny. Here are described the citizens of the "kingdom" He proclaimed.

The style of subsequent teachings in the Sermon on the Mount is dominated by the *imperative* calling us to decision and action. The Beatitudes with their startling *declarations* stimulate reflection and self-examination.

When Jesus says "poor in spirit," does He speak of me? Am I among the meek who shall inherit the earth? Am I a peacemaker? Am I merciful? If these are the qualities of those who shall "inherit" the kingdom of God, are they the qualities that mark my life? These are the questions which arise within us as we read the Beatitudes.

It is no accident that the Sermon on the Mount should begin by thrusting us back upon ourselves in earnest self-examination. Too many of us hope and work in a vague sort of way for a better world without first coming to terms with ourselves. And yet what is most deeply wrong with the world is often but a reflection of what is most inwardly wrong with each of us.

In the room above me as I write these lines is an elderly man who recently came seeking help. For many years he was a political activist, spending his energies in many "righteous" causes. He has noble thoughts about the kind of world this should be. Yet his own life is filled with confusion. Twice married and divorced he is now almost totally alienated from relatives and friends.

What about you?

Are you too filled with high ideals and noble aspirations, but unwilling to face up to the weaknesses in yourself?

B. Study

The Beatitudes, as suggested above, call us to self-examination. In the following study, attached to each Beatitude, are questions and comments intended to stimulate such a process of self-examination. You will also find the questions listed together in the appendix. Using these questions as a guide, read the Beatitudes. Write down the thoughts that come to you. This is very important. *Write out* your thoughts. It will help you to be concrete and clear. Then share your answers to the questions for self-examination with those with whom you are studying.

1. "Blessed are the poor in spirit, for theirs is the kingdom of heaven" (Matthew 5:3).

Do I have exaggerated notions of myself? Can I recall times and events when it became painfully clear to me that I was thinking more highly of myself than I should have? Do I want to break free from pride and know myself as I truly am?

The New English Bible translates this first Beatitude: "How blest are those who know they are poor. . . ." This is a free translation, but an inspired one. For Jesus in this first beatitude is speaking about humility, and there is no better definition of humility than "to know that we are poor." Humility, or poverty of spirit, is not a matter of thinking low thoughts about ourselves. It is not a matter of groveling in the dust. It is simply a matter of knowing ourselves as we really are.

And when we see ourselves as we really are, we will see that we are poor.

The opposite of spiritual poverty is pride. In pride we think more highly of ourselves than the truth will allow. One of the great curses hanging over the world is that men and nations are almost always tending to think more highly of themselves than they ought.

In pride we apply to ourselves gifts and powers we do not have. In pride we assume an exaggerated role in our families, our circle of friends, our occupation, our society. In pride we hide from our faults and sins, and display our virtues. In pride we assign ourselves a place in history which does not belong to us.

Even when I am seemingly broken and lacking all self-confidence, it is possible that I am consumed by pride. My lack of self-confidence, it turns out, is a fruit of a completely false idea of myself. I will not accept myself for what I am. I want to play a role beyond my capacity. Discouragement and joylessness are frequently the fruit of pride.

Few of us escape the trap of pride. In a growing number of people in our time pride has assumed pathological proportions. Children raised in a home situation where the parents do not love one another may develop particular problems. Sometimes in such a home the mother will form a special attachment to her son. She tries to make up in her relationship to her child what she misses in her relationship to her husband. When this happens it has terrible effects on the child. At a time when her son should receive training as a child, he is being treated as a companion. Because the mother needs the son's affection she does not see him in a clear objective light. She fails to discipline him. She does not cultivate in him a proper sense of himself. She makes too much of him. She instills in him exaggerated notions. The son, slowly learning that the mother needs him, learns also how to use the mother's need to get what he wants. He becomes a manipulator. He gets his own way by subtle forms of persuasion, intimidation, and outright argument. His success in manipulating the adult world breeds in him a contempt for others. He becomes grandiose about his own ideas. He begins playing a role that is much beyond his age or capacities. These and other even more terrible things can happen in such a situation.

The same thing can happen between a daughter and her father, and in other familial relationships.

If you are the child of such a home, you should look with special earnestness into what may have happened to you. Painful as it may be, and difficult, you will never find a fully purposeful life, or discover your place in the "kingdom of God," until you break free from the deeply imbedded pride that may have been instilled into you.

But how can we break free from pride? How can we become poor in spirit? How can we come to a true knowledge of our poverty? All of us from time to time receive intimations of our pride. It may be something small. I can remember distinctly how my pride became evident to me on one occasion in connection with a game of volleyball. I thought I was one of the better players. The team captain made it clear to me that my estimate was clearly out of focus by letting me sit on the sidelines during the crucial parts of the game. Or pride may be revealed to us in some enormously crushing experience: the breaking up of a marriage, failure on a job, or bondage to some obviously destructive sin. In these and many other ways we are suddenly confronted with our "poverty."

Whether small or large, these intimations of pride, or glimpses of reality, as we might call them, are from the hand of God. By them God tries to open us up to the reality of ourselves, of the world around us, and ultimately of Himself.

At such moments of self-revelation a critical question faces us, perhaps the most critical of our lives: Do we want to know the reality of the world we live in and do we want to see God and His sphere of power and glory, His kingdom? Do we want it so badly that we welcome the death of our inflated self? Our answers to these questions may determine whether or not we break free from pride and "inherit the kingdom of God."

2. "Blessed are those who mourn, for they shall be comforted" (Matthew 5:4).

Am I quick to mourn when I do wrong? Have I confessed my sins, or are there mis-

deeds that I am still trying to hide from my-
self, from God, and from others? Do I sorrow
deeply for my sins? Or do I pass over them
in a quick and superficial manner?

Jesus came preaching repentance, change, a turning away from wrong, and a turning toward God and the good. We may assume, therefore, that the mourners of whom He speaks in this second beatitude are those gripped by the agony of repentance. And repentance, true repentance, is an agony.

There is a direct connection between poverty of spirit and the mourning which Jesus speaks about here. The poor in spirit, as we have seen, are those who know how poor they are. They have dropped their defenses. They are no longer trying to hide from themselves. When they do this they come face-to-face with their sins and weaknesses. Such an encounter produces sorrow. If it is the right kind of sorrow, it will lead to contrite confession, forgiveness, and consolation.

> "A broken and a contrite heart, O God,
>   Thou wilt not despise."

Psalm 51:17

In our mental hospitals there are patients suffering from a disorder called hebephrenia. Patients afflicted by hebephrenia spend hours and hours of their waking day laughing, smirking, and giggling. Superficially it would seem they are happy, but there are few conditions that are more tragic, for the hebephrenic patient rarely recovers. He has fled from

28

reality to the extreme. The giddy world of his imagination seals him off from the dark problems that assail him. Paradoxically, it may seem, there is far more hope for the patient in deep depression. His depression is a sign in most cases that he is in contact with the reality of his life. His profound sadness, it turns out, is not without reason, and if followed by repentance and confession can be a stepping-stone on the way to a joyous end.

There are many people outside of mental institutions who react to their sins like the hebephrenic. They try to cover them up. They try to forget them by hiding them under a thin cloak of superficial gaiety. It is astonishing how many people in our time are struggling within themselves over some unconfessed sin.

What about you? Is there some secret sin that you are struggling with? Do you shrink back from the painful guilt and shame of it? Let sorrow have its way. Make a frank confession to God and some other trusted friend. If others have been affected by your sin, do not hold back from confessing to them. Stand ready to make restitution if that is necessary and possible. When Jesus came into the home of Zacchaeus, Zacchaeus stood and said, "Behold, Lord, the half of my goods I give to the poor; and if I have defrauded any one of anything, I restore it fourfold" (Luke 19:8).

For the future covet a clear conscience. Learn to live, as someone has said, with short accounts. Settle quickly with the charges that conscience brings against you. You will find consolation. Your life will be filled with peace and joy.

3. "Blessed are the meek, for they shall inherit the earth" (Matthew 5:5).

Do I have a settled faith and trust in God? Do I love God's will?

When in our poverty of spirit and repentant sorrow we look beyond ourselves to God to be mastered by His will, then we are meek. After forty years in the wilderness Moses had become a meek man. Before that he was a typical revolutionary. He saw the oppression and in anger slew the oppressor. But soon after this he had to flee into the wilderness. There he learned humility and meekness. There he learned to listen for the will of God.

Today the meek man is caricatured. He is frequently pictured as a henpecked husband. There is a partial truth in this picture. The henpecked husband is overpowered. Unfortunately, the one who overpowers him is his wife. But, nevertheless, it can be said that the meek men who will one day inherit the earth are men overpowered by another. That other, however, is God.

In the Greek language a donkey, broken and trained, can be spoken of as a meek animal. The meek man is broken and trained by God.

The New English Bible translates this word "meek" with the word "gentle." "How blest are those of a gentle spirit." Gentleness, to be sure, is a fruit of meekness. But the main point about the meek is not their gentleness but their quiet faith and trust in God. The meek turn again and again to God, for help, for direction, and for the sheer joy of it.

Pause here for a moment. Have you grasped the meaning of these first three beatitudes? Have you written down the thoughts that have come to you as you have meditated on them? Is there any thought that has come to you which you have pushed aside, perhaps because it is too painful to face? It may be just that suppressed memory that holds the key to your future peace.

Consider that Jesus attaches to these three beatitudes the greatest promises imaginable. What could be greater than to live on this earth ("They shall inherit the earth"), full of joy ("They shall be comforted"), and experiencing every day the reality of God's kingdom ("Theirs is the kingdom of heaven"). These great promises are made to those who humble themselves, experience the sorrow of repentance, and learn to do God's will.

4. "Blessed are those who hunger and thirst for righteousness, for they shall be satisfied" (Matthew 5:6).

For what am I hungering and thirsting? What concerns lie at the center of my life? Do I have a strong desire to see a more just and loving life among men on this earth?

31

With this fourth beatitude we come to the crowning mark of the inner life of the kingdom citizen: his hunger for righteousness.

The term "righteousness" has fallen into disrepute both inside and outside of Christian circles in our time. When people today think of righteousness, more often than not they think of self-righteousness. They think of stern-faced moralists striving to be good along some very narrow and often meaningless lines. The image of the joyless Puritan has cast a shadow over our thinking about righteousness.

Jesus knew about this kind of righteousness. In fact, the underlying purpose of the teaching of Jesus in the Sermon on the Mount is to combat this false variety of righteousness by upholding a new righteousness. "For I tell you," Jesus says in verse 20 of this same chapter, "unless your righteousness exceeds that of the scribes and Pharisees, you will never enter the kingdom of heaven."

It is this higher righteousness that Jesus has in mind when He speaks of the blessedness of those who hunger and thirst for it. This is not the place for a full and detailed discussion of this righteousness. It is enough here to recall that under the impact of Jesus' teaching we have come to replace the word "righteousness" with the word "love." Jesus is speaking here about those who hunger and thirst for a life marked by love in the fullest and strongest sense of that word.

With this in mind it should be noted that Jesus speaks here of our *hunger* and *thirst* for love. The crowning mark of the inner life of the new men described here is not that they do in fact act righteously. It is not said that they are in fact loving, or that they are rich in loving deeds. All that is important. But what is emphasized here is that they hunger for righteousness. They thirst for a more loving life.

This beatitude prompts a look at our heart's desire. What hungers and desires operate within us? Which of them commands our utmost loyalty? There are many gods contending for enthronement within each of us: the physical appetites, wealth, honor, family. The list is familiar. But there is also another power within us contending for allegiance and that is the still small voice prompting us to a more loving life. This voice is the voice of the living God, for God is love. Are you serving this God above all others?

If you are, Jesus promises, you will be satisfied. All the other powers and forces within will find their rightful place, and our inner life will radiate a joyful harmony. We will find the humane and loving life we long for.

> Humility
> Repentant sorrow
> Meekness
> Hunger for a loving life

These, then, are the leading characteristics of the inner life of those whom Jesus called blessed in the first four beatitudes.

The characteristics mentioned in the final

four beatitudes may be seen as fruits of these first four:

So, for example, the humble man, open to his faults and failings, his defenses down and possessing a growing awareness of how poor he really is (first beatitude), will no longer stand in lofty judgment of others, but will begin to show the fruits of mercy and compassion in human relations (fifth beatitude).

The man who has undergone the painful process of facing up to his sins, confessing them and turning from them (second beatitude), will discover a new freedom to live openly and honestly with others and act with sincerity (purity of heart) in all that he does (sixth beatitude).

The man who has ceased living by his own selfish impulses, but seeks instead that which is willed by a loving God (third beatitude) will also possess the necessary detachment to mediate helpfully in the conflicts that ravage man's interpersonal life (seventh beatitude).

Finally, and most obviously, the man whose life orientation is governed by a desire for righteousness and love (fourth beatitude) will not shrink back at the point where he is called upon to suffer "for righteousness' sake," but will rather take his stand all the more joyfully, knowing that persecutions are frequently the fate of "prophets" and "disciples" and their patient endurance leads to a "rich reward" (eighth beatitude).

5. "Blessed are the merciful, for they shall obtain mercy" (Matthew 5:7).

Do I forgive those who wrong me? Or do I enjoy holding grudges and complaints against others? Do my compassions go out to those in difficult circumstances? Or do I reject the unlovely and the unlikable?

6. "Blessed are the pure in heart, for they shall see God" (Matthew 5:8).

Am I sincere? Are my motives pure? Do my actions spring from my heart and reflect who I know myself to be? Am I just one thing, outwardly and inwardly? Or am I divided and hypocritical?

7. "Blessed are the peacemakers, for they shall be called sons of God" (Matthew 5:9).

Am I effective in promoting peace and reconciliation? Where I am present are human relations made smoother, more loving? Or do problems needlessly multiply and petty contentions arise?

8. "Blessed are those who are persecuted for righteousness' sake, for theirs is the kingdom of heaven" (Matthew 5:10).

Do I stand up for the right, even when it costs me something? Do I accept joyfully the hardships that come as a consequence of my loyalty to Jesus and His way?

There is a vital interconnection between all the Beatitudes. If you find yourself failing in one, you should look carefully to see whether you might not be failing in others. If you shrink back from taking a stand for the right, perhaps it is because you are hungering for something other than righteousness. And if hunger for righteousness does not fill your life, perhaps it is because you have allowed some secret sin to lodge there. And if you are so open to sin, may it not be because you harbor a proud, discontented attitude toward life?

Again, if you find strife springing up around you, if you find yourself alienating people, should you not consider whether the fault may lie in your never having discovered the secret of meekness? Is there not too much self-will in you and not enough listening to others and to God? And does not that lead right back to your lack of humility?

The Beatitudes are ended, but Jesus adds two ecstatic declarations and several warnings directed to the men described in the Beatitudes.

9. "You are the salt of the earth" (Matthew 5:13).

Jesus is passionately certain that the men described in the Beatitudes are the men the world needs. Their presence will transform the earth, not in the violent way of wars and military revolutions, but with a quiet penetrating power. Like salt and light!

It is evident that Jesus in the saying about salt is thinking about taste, for He goes on to say, "But if salt has lost its taste. . . ." Salt seasons. It brings out the flavor. It livens up the food.

Men of the character described by Jesus in the Beatitudes bring life to the world around them. A disciple is not a dull, insipid creature.

There is a warning here, however. Salt may lose its flavor. If it does, it is impossible to restore it. Then it is good for nothing except to be thrown out to make footpaths.

It is no use, however, trying to *be* salt, or trying to avoid the fate of saltless salt. It is no use trying to season the situations around us. Salt is what we are, if we are the kind of men and women Jesus describes in the Beatitudes. The world *will* be salted and seasoned, if there are in it such people. If not, it will lose its taste, and no reforms or revolutions will basically alter the situation.

10. "You are the light of the world" (Matthew 5:14).

In the words of Jesus here we catch a glimpse of high expectations. Jesus anticipated that the kind of men described in the Beatitudes would be rich in "good works." It is these good works to which He is referring when He speaks of their being the light of the world. "Let your light so shine before men, that they may see your good works. . . ."

Again it is not a question of producing this light. Jesus does not admonish His disciples to *be* the light of the world. He does not call them to do good works. Rather, as we become the kind of men and women described in the Beatitudes, the good works will naturally follow. Out of the spirit of poverty, repentance, meekness, and love, in the midst of mercy, purity, peacemaking, and suffering, great deeds will be wrought. We ourselves will recognize these works as not of our own doing. In moments of humility and meekness and faith we become the instrument of God's creative action. All this will certainly happen.

The danger is not that there will be no good works, but that we will fail to let the works be seen. In order for the works to illuminate the world, they must become visible. This may fail to happen if the disciples separate themselves from others. Rather, we are challenged to live openly in the midst of the world, in close human contact with other people, so that the light of our accomplishments may shine forth to the glory of God.

IV

Our Life with Others

(Matthew 5:17-48)

A. Introduction

Beginning with Matthew 5:17 we come to a new section of the Sermon on the Mount. From this point in the Sermon to the end of chapter 5 we have a series of commandments, observations, and insights, challenging us to a new way of life in our relations with other people.

In these verses Jesus addresses us again and again with imperatives: "But I say to you. . . . Leave your gift. . . . Make friends quickly with your accuser. . . . Pluck it out. . . . Do not swear at all. . . . Do not resist. . . . Love your enemies. . . ." Interspersed among the imperatives are warnings and insights.

The Beatitudes brought us into contact with the *psychological insight* of Jesus, His ability to visualize a new man. In these verses we encounter the *moral insight* of Jesus, His passionate will to create a new society.

If the appropriate response to the Beatitudes is self-examination, the response called forth by these challenging warnings, observations, and imperatives is decision.

Several assumptions underlie words of this kind, assumptions that would hardly need to be discussed, were they not so often challenged in our time.

1. The Need for Guidance

One such assumption is that we do need guidance in human relationships. We need specific counsel as to how to live together with others. It is not enough to say that everyone should love God and follow his own conscience. A pure love for God would indeed show us the right way in our relations with our fellowmen, but we do not know how to love God in a pure way. The fact is that most of us are morally and spiritually immature. We may have mastered some of the superficial arts of socializing but we know very little about the deeper issues of life. Jesus gave the guidance found in these paragraphs because He knew how much His disciples would need it.

Many Christians are confused on this point. They have been told that in the Old Testament we have law, but in the New Testament we have freedom from the law. "In Christ," they have heard it said, we have progressed beyond the need for commandments and moral advice. This is not true. In the writings of Paul, where we can find suggestions of this kind, it is not the Old Testament and the New which Paul contrasts but his experience of the

Old Testament *as a Pharisee* and his experience *in Christ.* In his astonishing discovery that Jesus was the Messiah Paul was set free from bondage to the laws of Israel as he had experienced it during his life as a trained Pharisaic scholar. At the same time Paul came under the "law of Christ" (1 Corinthians 9:21; Galatians 6:2). In place of the life-stultifying disciplines he had known as a Pharisee, the teachings of Jesus had come into his life as a new and liberating force.

In all this Paul is only being faithful to the example of Jesus. Jesus criticized the Pharisees for their perverting the "law and the prophets" and pointed to the artificial legalism they had erected around the Scriptures. But this did not mean that Jesus thought moral instruction was unnecessary. The point that Jesus makes against the Pharisees is not that they give moral instruction and subject people to laws. What He asserts is that the Pharisaic vision of goodness is too narrow, too constricted. "Unless your righteousness *exceeds* that of the scribes and Pharisees, you will never enter the kingdom of God." In place of the burdensome and oftentimes petty and meaningless disciplines of Pharisaism Jesus offered His own "well-fitting" yoke. "Bend your necks to my yoke, learn from me. . . . For my yoke is good to bear, my load is light" (Matthew 11:29, 30, NEB).

If we examine the teachings of Jesus to discover the differences between His "yoke" and that of the Pharisees, we learn, for one thing, that Jesus goes much deeper into the spirit or intention of conduct than did the Pharisees. Not just the external act but the inner motive was the target of His concern. "There is nothing outside a man which by going into him can defile him," He said on one occasion, "but the things which come out of a man are what defile him" (Mark 7:15). Words such as these created the impression that Jesus was anti-law.

But this is specifically and strongly denied in the words which open this section of the Sermon on the Mount: "Think not that I have come to abolish the law and the prophets; I have come not to abolish them but to fulfill them" (Matthew 5:17). By going behind the letter of the law to its inner intention Jesus did not mean to annul the law but sought rather to help us grasp and act upon it in an even more radical and meaningful sense.

Another difference between the guidance that Jesus gave and that of the Pharisees can be seen in the distinction He drew between passing human opinions, customs, and traditions and the far more significant "commandments of God." Jesus charged the Pharisees with neglecting the weightier matters of the law in favor of the traditions of men. Mark 7:1-23. Rather humorously He pictured them as straining out gnats and swallowing camels! Matthew 23:24. This sometimes absurd lack of proportion among the religious leaders of His time

42

expressed itself especially in their observance of the Sabbath.

An enormous complex of regulations had arisen in Israel in relation to what was allowed and not allowed in the celebration of this day. Jesus swept them all aside with His liberating observation: "The sabbath was made for man, not man for the sabbath" (Mark 2:27). This is but one illustration of the way in which the whole field of human conduct is clarified by His piercing insight into the "royal law of love" (James 2:8; Mark 12:28-34). Had Jesus left us laws concerning customs, dress, food, days, and seasons, laws having to do with peripheral matters, His teaching would have passed away with the passing of the ancient culture in which He lived.

The greatness and novelty of Jesus' teaching lies in large part in the unerring wisdom with which He swept aside the petty and the time-bound traditions of His age, enabling His generation and the generations since, regardless of cultural circumstances, to come face-to-face with those issues that truly determine life and death. In Him and His teachings the will of God shines upon our world with unusual brightness and intensity.

To repeat: Underlying this section of Jesus' teaching is the assumption that we do indeed need guidance in the realm of human relations. Our decision to follow Jesus and seek His kingdom does not automatically make us wise in human affairs. We must listen to what

He says. We must allow Him to teach us.

2. *The Need to Be Challenged*

A second and related assumption undergirding the teachings here is that we not only need counsel, but we need that counsel in a form that sharply challenges us. It is not only the content of the teaching that is striking but the form. Jesus does not address us in these verses like some elderly wise man giving us advice. He speaks to us rather as a prophet, with the sharpest imperatives and warnings. And the assumption is that we need to be addressed in this way. We need more than guidance as to how to relate to others; we need that guidance in a form that awakens us, that stimulates our will to action.

It is necessary to emphasize this point because neither outside nor inside the churches today are we accustomed to hearing this kind of speech. We live in an era of permissiveness. Moral imperatives are out of style. Modern man is reluctant to accept the authority of another in the realm of human behavior. He is comfortable only with a rational or experiential approach to moral guidance. He will listen to "advice," providing it is couched in reasoned terms and is nonbinding. One of the most widespread theories of counseling in our time maintains that most people have already too many moral restraints binding them. Man must be set free from these restraints so that he can evolve his own values. According to this theory there is within every man the capacity to bring forth a sound and wholesome way of life, if only we allow him the freedom to do so.

There is an element of truth in all this. I cite these examples not to discredit them completely, but only to suggest a contrast to what we find in the teachings of this section of the Sermon on the Mount. Clearly the words of Jesus here assume that we do need an authority in the realm of human relations, someone beyond ourselves who will give us firm direction. Our will, our moral imagination, is lazy and corrupt. Our capacity for decision needs awakening.

B. Study

In approaching the Beatitudes we directed our attention to certain questions for self-examination. The Beatitudes, we suggested, awaken this kind of response. In this second section of the teachings we are faced with a very different kind of challenge. Jesus' words here thrust us away from ourselves to others. The appeal is to decision in the realm of social life. This calls for a different style of study and response. In approaching this section of teaching we will try to clarify the point of Jesus' challenge, and engage in an act of decision with regard to it. One way of doing this is by means of a covenant.

A covenant is a solemn statement of agreement between two or more parties. In the story of God's people recorded in the Bible covenants play a large and important role.

When God brought Israel out of Egypt, He established a covenant with His people at Mount Sinai. This covenant is recorded in the so-called Decalogue in Exodus 20 and Deuteronomy 5. The Decalogue begins by telling what God has done for His people (Exodus 20:2), and then specifies what God wants by way of obedience (Exodus 20:3-17). The covenant is established when the people agree to practice "all that the Lord has spoken" (Exodus 24:7).

As a way of responding to this section of the Sermon on the Mount, we have formulated such a covenant based on the teachings of Jesus in Matthew 5:21-48. In this covenant we try to make as explicit as possible the terms of our responsibility as disciples of Jesus in relation to our life with others. *You will find this covenant statement at the conclusion of this section of our study, as well as in the appendix.*

Before turning to this covenant, however, it is important to look at the teachings of Jesus themselves and try to understand as fully as possible their bearing on various life relationships. The following comments are meant to assist you in this process. Read them as a stimulant to your own thought and meditation.

Five distinct, critical issues in human relationships are dealt with by Jesus in Matthew 5:17-48:

      1. Anger (5:21-26)
      2. Lust (5:27-32)

3. False speech (5:33-37)
4. Retaliation (5:38-42)
5. Enemy hatred (5:43-48)

These five issues touch on relationships among those within the Christian community, as well as on the way this community relates to the sometimes evil and destructive world around it. In its actual formulation the teaching may seem negative, but its thrust is in the direction of a life characterized by peace, purity, truthfulness, and overpowering love.

Let us look more closely at each of the five issues.

1. *Concerning Anger* (Matthew 5:21-26)

Jesus makes it clear that He wants His disciples free from anger. He speaks in this passage of the "brother." He is talking about the community of His disciples. He wants those who belong to this society not only to cease murdering one another, but also to stop all angry outbursts and destructive insults.

The anger spoken of here is the emotion that lies behind murder. It is destructive. It despises the brother, belittles him, and hurts him. It is blind and lethal. Such anger rends the fabric of human relations and wounds those it touches.

Many people today take a hard attitude against murder but a very lenient one toward anger. The outbursts of anger sometimes seen in men in high office are considered the mark of a robust personality. Many psychological counselors encourage their clients to accept their anger as a normal part of a healthy personality and to express it in appropriate ways.

When we are angry we should, of course, acknowledge it. Many people find themselves caught in situations where they harbor angry, hostile feelings toward those who are supposedly near and dear to them. They find it impossible to face up to their true feelings. As a consequence they repress their anger, even denying it to themselves. They compound their anger with self-deception. It is necessary in such instances to encourage a clear recognition of the truth of the situation. If a person is angry, there is no virtue in hiding it. In fact, by hiding it we lose the power to deal with it.

But deal with it we must. Jesus warns us in the most vigorous way against any inclination we might have to minimize the seriousness of anger. It can bring us to hell, He says, and anyone who has seen an otherwise lovely personality corrupted by recurrent attacks of anger knows that His warning is not without reason. Anger is temporary madness, and has no place in the life of the Christian community.

This matter is of such importance that Jesus adds to His words of warning about anger some very practical directions as to how its presence in the company of disciples may be diminished. There are two procedures (verses 23-26) which Jesus wants put into practice wherever His disciples are together. These procedures, if adhered to, will greatly reduce the possibility of anger ever getting a foothold in the community of brothers in the first place.

First, clear up offenses done against another just as soon as you become aware of them. Even if on the way to something as important as the worship of God you should suddenly think of an action done to another that might have caused offense, stop immediately, go, and confess the fault and make it right again. Be quick to admit your wrong and prompt to deal with its consequences, especially when the offense of another is at stake. Not only your sin is involved, but by your straightforwardness you may protect your brother from falling into the pitfall of anger.

Second: "Make friends quickly with your accuser" (5:25). In these words Jesus visualizes the *offended* party as taking the initiative. That can be the occasion for an even more explosive situation than the previous one so far as anger is concerned. When *I* become aware of having offended someone and set out to make it right the battle is virtually won, but when the offended one, my accuser, comes first to me, the moment is ripe for anger. Do not let it happen! Do not let charges and countercharges hang fire. Reestablish the bond of fraternity at once. "*Make friends quickly* with your accuser."

Here are some very practical words about

a most difficult problem in human relations. Jesus offers them to us as a matter of decision for every disciple. Will you or will you not take a stand against angry feelings? Will you or will you not act promptly to clear up the wrongs you may have done to another? Will you or will you not settle promptly the accusations brought against you? Jesus challenges us to take anger seriously, purge it from our midst, and do those things that make it difficult for anger to arise.

2. *Concerning Lust* (Matthew 5:27-32)

Jesus speaks here about adulterous lust and its frightful consequences: divorce, broken homes, displaced women and children, and multiple marriages. Just as He wanted the community of His disciples free from murder and anger, so He wants it free from adultery, in thought as well as deed. He also speaks out against divorce. His words are meant in the first place for men ("everyone who looks at a woman lustfully"), and married men in particular. By extension they apply to the whole realm of relationships between men and women.

The teachings of Jesus on divorce (5:31, 32) have occasioned much controversy. The force and direction of His thoughts on this subject, however, are beyond dispute. Like the prophets of old He clearly rejected the shallow legalism that allowed a man to dissolve his marriage at whim by means of a slip of paper. His words echo the cry of Malachi: "I hate putting away" (Malachi 2:16). "Every one who divorces his wife and marries another commits adultery" (Luke 16:18). Words such as these are not meant to legislate for all the complex marital tangles that present themselves to the church. Even less are they intended as the basis of legislation in a state or society made up of Christians as well as non-Christians. They must rather be understood as a vehement protest against the conduct of selfish, adulterous men who bring untold sufferings to their wives and children by their divorces and multiple marriages. They are spoken in passionate defense of fidelity in marriage.

In the fight against adultery Jesus calls for self-discipline. "If your right eye causes you to sin, pluck it out. . . . If your right hand causes you to sin, cut it off" (Matthew 5:29, 30). This, of course, is not meant literally. The removal of the right eye or the right hand physically would still leave us with the left eye and hand, both of which are equally capable of adulterous lust. What Jesus does mean is that He wants His disciples to deal decisively in this area. They must put an end to adulterous thinking and fantasizing. They must reject without compromise any thought of extramarital affairs. To yield to adulterous passions is to risk the descent of our "whole body" into "hell." Such are Jesus' sharp warnings to married men.

Unmarried disciples reading these words will naturally ask: What relevance does this teaching have for us? It is also obvious that we are living in a time when deviant sexual conduct such as fornication, pornography, masturbation, and homosexuality is widespread and in some instances on the increase. What bearing, if any, do Jesus' words concerning adultery have on such practices as these, as well as on the general loosening of sexual standards in our time?

In applying Jesus' sexual teachings more broadly it is important to emphasize the unique significance He attached to marriage as the goal of sexuality. This point is clearly implied in the teachings on adultery we have already examined, but it must be underscored, in order not to lose sight of the very positive attitude toward sexual life that permeates His teachings. Christianity is sometimes interpreted as taking a negative attitude toward sexual life. This is certainly not the case so far as Jesus Himself is concerned. There is not a line of His teaching that depreciates sex or ranks sexual life below celibacy as a way of discipleship. Rather His teaching on this subject expresses an earnestness and a will to see this side of life reach its highest and most mature fulfillment within the covenant of marriage (see Matthew 19:4-6).

Seen in this light many sexual deviations must be judged as harmful as adultery itself. The person enslaved by pornography, for example, conjures up a world of depersonalized sex objects around which fantasies of fornication and adultery are spun. This fantasizing process, Jesus said, can be as personally destructive as the act itself. It may even be more destructive, for to the sin of adultery is added the sin of make-believe, self-containment, and isolation. This is the opposite of marriage where sexual love is a shared experience between two real people.

Masturbation presents a similar problem. This may seem relatively harmless, and no doubt is, as a passing phase of adolescent experimentation. But here too a life experience meant to unite us deeply with another person is turned into a private, self-stimulated pleasure. When retained and practiced as an adult way of sexual life it reinforces the self-centeredness and self-preoccupation of a personality already all too often turned in upon itself. As such it almost inevitably brings with it a lack of self-respect and a sense of inadequacy and not infrequently leads to a bondage to sensual experience that permeates the whole personality.

Obviously neither pornography nor masturbation prepares a person to live in the real world of responsible sexuality as experienced in a genuinely loving marriage. Although no longer considered the vices they once were, they cannot be seen otherwise than as incompatible with the thinking of Jesus. Needless to say the same must be said about homosexuality, where the God-given purpose in sexuality is completely misdirected, as those know only too well who are bound by this perversion. When able to face the truth, homosexuals will admit to a profound hostility toward those they supposedly "love" in this way.

As with adultery those tempted by such distorted sexual practices will have to take decisive action if they expect to find freedom for a more mature sexual life. The first and hardest step in attaining such freedom may well involve sharing the problem with someone else. Sin wants us alone, Dietrich Bonhoeffer has written. By ourselves we are especially vulnerable to distortion, exaggeration, and excuses. By ourselves it is hard to see our problems in their true proportions. This is especially true where sexual sins are involved, surrounded as they often are by an especially charged atmosphere of secrecy, guilt, and fear. But shared with others who know the love and power of God and who can speak both of forgiveness and consolation, as well as challenge and warning, their strength over us diminishes, and courage for a more responsible sexuality can be won.

A more difficult issue is coming to the fore in our time in the growing acceptance of sexual intimacy between unmarried men and women. Even within the Christian church there is a gradual concession to the spirit of the times on this matter. The argument is increasingly heard that such sexual expression is legitimate, even wholesome, where the persons involved have genuine affection for one another and are not just out to exploit each other selfishly. Such teaching ignores the testimony of Israel (Deuteronomy 22:20), of Jesus (Matthew 15:19), and of the early church (1 Corinthians 6:9, 10; Galatians 5:19; Ephesians 5:3, 5). It also runs counter to experience. Those who experiment in this direction soon discover that the sexual act, torn from the context of a secure, lifelong covenant, cannot satisfy its deepest intent. Even if children are not generated, the sexual act itself produces a profound sense of marital and familial love which is more difficult for women to suppress than for men. Where such instinctive feelings are repressed for the sake of sexual freedom, those involved may find themselves on the road to emotional instability and emptiness. Random premarital sexual intercourse, even between those who think they love each other at the time, is obviously no preparation for a faithful and loving monogamous marriage. There can be no doubt that a society encouraging this will also witness the gradual breakdown of marriage, with all the consequent social and emotional disasters already seen on every hand.

Is there no place then in the life of the unmarried disciple for sexual expression? Does he have nothing to look forward to in this area but a hard denial of his sexual feelings? There is a growing protest in our time against a Puritanical attitude toward sex, which would try to deal with this area of life by denying its existence. This protest is legitimate. We only deceive ourselves if we do not face up to the way sexuality is woven into the whole fabric of our existence. God made us male and female and pronounced us good. It would be wrong therefore to try to escape sexuality. Men should be manly, women womanly, and both should rejoice in the emotional richness this polarity brings to their relationships. In this sense no one lives without sexuality.

At the same time it is clear that the unmarried, who would be faithful to Jesus, must practice self-denial when it comes to overt sexual expression. Sexual intercourse is reserved for those in a marriage covenant. This is the only conclusion we can draw from the teachings of Jesus, from the prophets and teachers of Israel, and from experience itself.

However, it needs to be said, in our time especially, that the lack of overt sexual experience in no way deprives a person of leading a fully human existence. It is not as though an essential human condition has been lost. Jesus Himself was unmarried and even suggested on one occasion that the future of man "in heaven" will be a future without marriage (Matthew 22:30).

Sexual life is good, but it is not the ultimate good which many devotees of Venus consider it to be. In fact, Jesus intimated on another occasion that there are those who will render special service to the kingdom of God through their celibate calling (Matthew 19:12). Their freedom from marital and parental responsibilities gives them a special liberty for serving others. The time of celibacy in a Christian's life should be seen as a gift, just as Christian marriage is a gift. It is an opportunity from the hand of God to tackle those tasks and dare those deeds that the marriage state does not allow. And in doing this the celibate will experience the joys of a life well lived.

In summary: Sexual experience is good, but it is not the highest good. Undisciplined, it carries within it the seeds of its own destruction. In the midst of a society increasingly bent on exploiting sex for selfish ends, Jesus calls us who would be His disciples to stand firmly against adultery and related sexual perversions in defense of lifelong monogamous marriage as the sphere of sexual intimacy and fulfillment.

3. *Concerning False Speech* (Matthew 5:33-37)

The third issue touched on by Jesus in this section of the Sermon on the Mount will require only a few comments. Here it would seem the imperatives have to do with what today might be called commercial or public relationships. The critical question in this realm is truthful speech. It remains one of the most urgent needs of public life to insure truth in the courts, truth in business, truth in the day-by-day commerce of people with one another. Societies continue to employ the oath as a way of supporting truth and discouraging the lie.

For disciples of Jesus, however, all that is

unnecessary. Here simple truth itself is the rule. Jesus wants us at all times to be direct, clear, and simple in our speech, saying what we mean, no more and no less. "Anything more than this comes from evil."

This is no easy task. There are many situations where truth is compromised almost by habit. In a hospital where I worked, twelve sick days were granted each year. They were meant to be used as sick days. I found it was only the rare employee who did not use them for other purposes and in the process falsify his timekeeping record. An even deeper problem are those social conventions that suggest we must behave in certain ways. They prevent us from really speaking what is on our hearts. If someone offends us, we do not speak to him about it, but put on a front of pleasantness. If we are guilty or ashamed of something, we do not confess it. We try to cover it up. Wherever people are together in such an untruthful way, the deeper springs of love and trust dry up.

It goes without saying that if Jesus requires of His disciples truthful speech in their life among the public, He requires it among themselves. This is already implied in His instructions about anger. He wants us to be straightforward with one another. This does not mean crude bluntness. Always the truth must be spoken in love, with tact and good will. But let it be the truth.

It requires an act of will to accomplish all this. We must take a stand for speaking the truth. Anyone who wants to be a disciple and participate in the life of the Christian fellowship must declare his earnest desire and intention to speak the truth from his heart.

4. *Concerning Retaliation* (Matthew 5:38-42)

The fourth issue taken up by Jesus in this section of the Sermon on the Mount focuses on the attitude of disciples toward those who wrong them. "Do not set yourself against the man who wrongs you" (NEB). In saying this Jesus completely rejected retaliation in any form as a pattern of conduct for His disciples and rendered obsolete the old "lex talionis," "an eye for an eye, and a tooth for a tooth." Realizing that such radical counsel as this would be understood by His hearers only with great difficulty, He went on to illustrate it. To this principle, four examples are appended, one from the realm of interpersonal relations ("if any one strikes you on the right cheek, turn to him the other also"), another from the realm of jurisprudence ("if any one would sue you and take your coat, let him have your cloak as well"), a third from the realm of politics ("if any one forces you to go one mile, go with him two miles"), and a fourth from the realm of business ("give to him who begs from you, and do not refuse him who would borrow from you").

This paragraph of the Sermon on the Mount has frequently been misinterpreted because of a failure to distinguish between principle and application. The only principle set forth here is the one stated at the very beginning: "Do not set yourself against the man who wrongs you" (NEB). In stating this principle Jesus follows a legal style as old as the Decalogue. Scholars refer to commandments formulated in this way as "apodictic" laws. Apodictic pronouncements or laws have a universal sweep to them. This ruling against retaliation is meant by Jesus to apply always and everywhere.

He is not talking here so much about enemies. That problem is taken up in the next and final paragraph of this section of the Sermon. He is talking rather about those many hurts and offenses that inevitably come our way, living as we do in a world filled with selfish, thoughtless people. In relation to such wrongs and those who perpetrate them, Jesus wants us free from revenge.

The principle, then, is that we should not retaliate. The four illustrations which Jesus adds to this principle suggest the range of its application. These illustrations are formulated not as apodictic laws, but as "case" laws. This too is a familiar legal style with many examples in the law codes of the Old Testament as well as throughout the ancient world. Case laws begin typically with an "if" clause: "if [in the case that] any one strikes you . . . if any one would sue you." Such laws refer to very specific cases. They are not meant to be universalized, but are themselves examples of the application of a larger principle. In the instances at hand they are examples of the one law that we should not retaliate. They illustrate how radically Jesus meant this commandment to guide us in all the various spheres of life where it applies.

For example, we should not strike back at the man who insults us, even if the insult is the most offensive one imaginable (the flick on the cheek). If pressed to law for our property, we should not bear a grudge against the one suing us, but deal generously with him. If conscripted into service by a policeman or soldier, or unjustly treated by some political power, we must maintain an attitude of good will, and go beyond the service demanded of us. The same must hold true in our relation to the man who tries to take advantage of us in financial matters. These are breathtaking illustrations of a revolutionary new spirit which Jesus wants to introduce into the sphere of human relations. Paul caught the significance of these statements when he instructed the Roman Christians not to be overcome by evil, but to overcome evil with good (Romans 12:21).

5. *Concerning Enemies* (Matthew 5:43-48)

We come finally to the fifth and last issue in human relations, the question of the disciples' relation to "enemies." There is no problem in our time more laden with potential disaster than the problem of enemies. This problem is written large on the current international scene. The larger nation states of our time seem to need an enemy for their existence. The psychology and energy of the nation are organized around the dread enemy. Now it is Japan, now Russia, now China, and whoever it may be, this enemy must be feared, plotted against, fought (if necessary), and hated.

What we see on the international scene, also operates on the level of interpersonal life. Many personalities seem to need an enemy to survive. They must have someone to blame, someone to fight. Children must blame their parents, workers their bosses, bosses their workers. This penetrates even into the church. Leaders struggle for power. They resent those who gain the upper hand. Sometimes where the atmosphere is unloving, the smallest thing can precipitate a spirit of enmity.

But Jesus commands us to stop all this. He doesn't close His eyes to the problem. Nor does He make any sweet promises. He offers no magical formulas for turning enemies into friends. He assumes that His disciples will have enemies like everyone else, perhaps even more than others, for they will have to endure, as He did, persecutions "for righteousness' sake." The only point He makes is that we should love these enemies. We should not just refrain from hating them. We should cultivate toward our enemies an inner attitude of good will, yes, even seeking the good of those who have gone so far as to do us bodily harm. We should pray for those who persecute us.

Jesus assumes this can be done. He is not

saying we should grow in love toward those who hate us. He is calling us to decision: Love your enemies!

It is astonishing how little attention the Christian church has paid to these instructions. When it comes to loving our enemies, the church is almost totally conformed to the times. In none of the countries where it exists has the church, with the exception of a small minority, been able to stand against the spirit of enemy hatred which poisons the international atmosphere. And internally the church is all too often rent by members who themselves are enemies and do not love one another.

All this must be seen as a great tragedy for the Christian movement, and especially so when one realizes that Jesus not only taught us to love our enemies but gave a supreme example of this love. To the dismay of His own first disciples He refused to organize violent resistance against those who plotted His death. Instead He allowed them to capture and crucify Him. The cross, so celebrated as a symbol in Christianity, is nothing less than the consequence of this nonviolent loving approach toward enemies.

With these words and this example before us, it must be said in the most unequivocal terms: Hatred of enemies and participation in fighting and wars, at whatever level they rage, is a violation of our Christian calling. If you want to follow Jesus, you must take up the cross, as He did, and suffer rather than retaliate, love and forgive rather than hate and destroy.

The following covenant, as previously indicated, is an attempt to summarize the thrust of Matthew 5:17-48. Does it accurately reflect Jesus' teaching in this section? Is it your desire to live by this covenant in your relations with others?

A COVENANT FOR CHRISTIAN DISCIPLES
Concerning Our Life with Others
Based on Matthew 5:17-48

In gratitude to God for all that I have come to know and experience through Jesus Christ, and in anticipation of His coming kingdom, I will gladly, with His help, try to uphold the following covenant:

1. *Concerning anger:* I will take a stand not only against murderous deeds, but against angry, destructive thoughts and emotions (5:21, 22), seeking first of all to purge them from my own life and taking care not to become the occasion for anger on the part of another, (a) by confessing and righting my wrongs against my brother *as soon as I become aware of them* (5:23, 24), and (b) by dealing forthrightly with all matters of conflict between myself and another *as soon as they are brought to my attention* (5:25, 26).

2. *Concerning sexual lust*: It is my intention not only to avoid an adulterous act but to stay free from adulterous thoughts (5:27-30), as

well as other sexual perversions. On the positive side I will uphold the standard of life-long marital love and fidelity (5:31, 32).

3. *Concerning false speech*: I will try under all circumstances to speak the truth in love, simply and clearly, and abide by my promises (5:33-37).

4. *Concerning retaliation:* I will guard against taking revenge against anyone who wrongs me or exchanging injury for injury (5:38, 39a). I will seek rather to overcome evil with good (5:39b-42; Romans 12:21).

5. *Concerning enemies:* I will not surrender to an attitude of hatred toward enemies. Instead, even though I suffer persecution at their hands, I will pray for them and seek their good (5:43-48).

V

Our Life with God

(Matthew 6)

A. Introduction

In chapter 6 the teachings of Jesus continue to confront us with sharp imperatives. In this section of the Sermon on the Mount, as in the previous one, we are called upon to be decisive. Here, however, the decisions called for have to do with a different set of issues than those dealt with in chapter 5. As we have seen, all the imperatives in chapter 5 have to do with *human* relations. In chapter 6 the dominant theme is our relationship to God. In this chapter we can gain insight into what it will mean to be a Christian disciple in the so-called religious domain.

Just as many Christians are ignorant of what Jesus taught about human relations, so they are ignorant of what He taught about our relations to God. It is astonishing how lightly people today call Him Lord, but ignore what He commanded us to do.

What does He command us to do so far as our relation to God is concerned?

In this chapter Jesus focuses on *three subjects*. In dealing with these three subjects He uncovers *two major problems*.

The three subjects are "Piety," "Prayer," and "Property."

"Piety," which we are using here as a term descriptive of certain stereotyped religious practices, is dealt with in verses 1-6 and 16-18.

This discussion of piety is interrupted by a section on "Prayer" in verses 7-15.

The remainder of the chapter is given over to a discussion of "Property," verses 19-34.

The two major problems uncovered by Jesus in dealing with these three subjects are: *Hypocrisy and Anxiety*. Hypocrisy is a special danger for those steeped in the pious practices of the synagogue (6:2, 5). Anxiety is a dominant characteristic of those whom Jesus refers to as "Gentiles" and has left its mark especially on their practice of prayer and their attitude toward material needs (6:7, 32).

B. Study

With this outline in mind, let us look more closely at each of the three major topics of this chapter: Piety, Prayer, and Property. Various study suggestions are interspersed through the following discussion. At the close of this section of our study you will find another covenant, summarizing, as did the previous one, the content of the chapter as a whole.

1. *Piety* (Matthew 6:1-6, 16-18)

"Beware of practicing your piety before men in order to be seen by them." This is the summons which opens this section of Jesus' teaching. The challenge is to "beware!" The issue under discussion requires our being on the alert. Why?

It is evident from other sayings of Jesus in the New Testament that few characteristics of the religious life of His time disturbed Him more than the insincerity of it (cf. His criticism of the scribes and Pharisees, Matthew 23). The religious side of life, it seems, is particularly vulnerable at this point. Expressions of religious devotion which at one time may be authentically meaningful become routine and stereotyped. In spite of this, they are retained as part of the "holy" tradition. We continue doing them because "that's the way things are done." From here to the point of doing them to be seen of men is a short step. In this way strongly held but essentially empty practices begin to dominate the religious life.

Three examples of "pious practices" capable of being perverted in this way are mentioned by Jesus in His teaching here: giving alms, prayer, and fasting. Religious men from time immemorial have given charity, conversed with God, and practiced various forms of self-discipline. Jesus does not criticize these practices as such. In fact, He more or less assumes that they will be a part of the life of His disciples as well. His disciples will give alms, they will pray, and they will fast. But while doing these things they will be on the alert against a very subtle danger: the danger of practicing these good deeds for their prestige value.

The following admonition, based on Jesus' words, attempts to pinpoint further the nature of this danger and how we can avoid it. Spend some time meditating on this admonition. Does it speak to anything in your life? Jot down your reactions and share them with your fellow disciples.

BE CAREFUL!
An Admonition Based on Matthew 6:1-6, 16-18

Be on your guard, disciple. Yes, you, precisely you who take your discipleship seriously, watch out! A special danger awaits you, lurking behind every good deed, hiding behind every sacrificial act, concealed within every noble prayer. This danger is so subtle and so hidden that you will not see it unless you look for it most carefully.

The danger is this: Parading your religion to be seen of men, seeking honor and praise from others through good deeds, gaining prestige through piety. This is not goodness; this is goody-goodness. It is laughable.* It is a mockery of true religion.

Therefore, when you do some act of charity, practice some self-discipline, or pray, be on

---

*In this passage we have an example of Jesus' humor. He is smiling at the foolish hypocrites.

your guard! No self-publicity! Do not even publicize your good deeds to yourself. ("Do not let your left hand know what your right hand is doing.") Become inwardly detached from your goodness and do not care whether anyone should ever see all the sacrifices you have made for God or for other people.

Begin thinking this way instead: God, my Father, sees and knows what I have done. That is enough. I want no other reward except the reward He has in store for me.

In summary: In our life with God, one of the great dangers is hypocrisy, pretending one thing while seeking another. This danger is especially great for the pious, those "in the synagogue," those steeped in religious traditions. The antidote to hypocrisy in religion is the cultivation of the real thing: the inward awareness and experience of the "Father who sees in secret." We must learn to live from this secret center. We must learn to love God with our whole being. We must learn to live for Him and the rewards He will give us and not worry about the praise or blame of others.

Again it should be emphasized, this is a matter for decision. True, there is also the phenomenon of growth, of becoming less concerned about the opinions of others, of becoming more aware of the favor or disfavor of God. But it is also a matter for decision, and that is what we find emphasized here. Jesus is challenging us. He is asking us to put forth an effort. Beware!

2. *Prayer and Property* (Matthew 6:7-15; 19-34)

Up to this point in the Sermon on the Mount Jesus has taught for the most part against the background of the prevailing Jewish religion of His time, that of the "scribes and Pharisees." In discussing the issues of prayer and property Jesus draws a contrast, not between the way of the scribes and Pharisees and that expected of His disciples, but between the attitudes of the "Gentiles" and those of His followers (6:7 and 6:32).

The attitude toward prayer and property among the "Gentiles" can be characterized by one word, *anxiety,* especially anxiety about physical needs.

It is this anxiety which drives the "Gentiles" on and on in their prayers. Imagining that the more they babble, the more they will get, and yet never certain of being heard, the prayers of the "Gentiles" are long and exhausting. Anxiety makes them that way.

It is this same anxiety that causes the "Gentiles" to worry about what they will eat and what they will wear. Because of this anxiety they jealously treasure whatever wealth they can accumulate against an uncertain future. In time these treasures absorb them, capture their "heart" (verse 21), and choke out everything else. As a consequence the "Gentiles" become selfish, narrow, and ruthless. They have no love for God. This is the darkness (6:23) from which Jesus would deliver us.

The key to our deliverance is contained in words twice repeated, once in connection with the discussion of prayer and once in the discussion of property: "Your Father knows what your needs are" (6:8). "Your heavenly Father knows that you need them all" (6:32, NEB).

A deeper awareness of the seeing God, that is Jesus' alternative to the hypocrisy of the Pharisees (6:6). *A deeper awareness of the knowing God* (6:8, 32), that is Jesus' alternative to the anxiety of the "Gentiles." God "sees" us and "knows" our needs! God is our Father and wants us for His sons! That is the good news that Jesus came preaching.

And once you hear it and accept it, you can find it confirmed all around you. Just look! Open your eyes to the lavish care poured out on even the most insignificant creatures. Look at the flowers of the field and the birds of the air. Look how marvelously they are clothed and equipped for their brief life. If these little creatures, here today and gone tomorrow, are so extravagantly cared for by God, *how much more* will He care for us!

If we would only let this sink in, if we would only listen to what Jesus is saying here and exercise more faith toward God and more confidence in His care for us, great

72

changes would come into our way of praying and our way of handling our property.

Let us look more closely at Jesus' teaching on these two subjects:

a. *Prayer* (Matthew 6:7-15)

Many people assume that all prayer is good. It is good to pray and bad not to pray. This is by no means the case. In this as in other areas we need to be taught. Even many Christians are still operating on a level with the "Gentiles" when it comes to prayer, simply because they have not taken the time to listen to what Jesus has to say. The first disciples said, "Lord, teach us to pray" (Luke 11:1). We should do likewise.

When we do, the first lesson we are taught is that God already knows our needs. Therefore, we do not need to exhaust ourselves reciting them in our prayers like the "Gentiles" do. Prayer rightly understood is not a matter of informing God of something He does not know. God already knows our needs better than we know them ourselves. That confidence is the foundation of Christian prayer.

But if God already knows what we need before we ask Him, why then pray at all? Does this not destroy the necessity of prayer altogether? It does, if prayer means nothing more to us than trying to get across our needs to God. But in the so-called "Lord's Prayer" Jesus suggests another kind of prayer.

"This is how you should pray," Jesus says

by way of preface to the Lord's Prayer. The "Lord's Prayer" is recited in Christian circles as a prayer in itself. But it is not at all certain that this was the intention of Jesus in giving us these lines. It would seem that these words were meant for instruction rather than recitation. They offer us suggestions as to the nature and subject matter of authentic prayer. If this is correct, instead of just repeating this prayer, we should take it and let it shape our whole way of communicating with God.

The following is an attempt to look at the "Lord's Prayer" from this standpoint. Read and discuss these suggestions. Put forth an effort to establish the priorities recommended here in your own prayer life. Report your experiences to one another in your study circle.

"THIS IS HOW YOU SHOULD PRAY"
Suggestions on How to Pray, Based on the Teachings of Jesus, Matthew 6:9-13

*"Our Father in heaven. . . ."*** Think of God as a loving, unseen, yet present Father, deeply aware and concerned about your needs, as well as the needs of your fellow disciples and those of the whole world. When you address God in prayer, say, "Father." This in itself is the first and greatest act of prayer, to turn from ourselves to the universe and

---

**NEB translation used throughout this study of the Lord's Prayer.

say, "Father," "Our Father." (Compare Romans 8:15; Galatians 4:6.)

"Thy name be hallowed. . . ." In prayer to God concentrate first of all on God Himself. Do not rush in with all your needs and wishes. He knows you and what you need before you ask Him, but you do not know Him. Quiet your heart and become aware of His greatness and goodness. Pray that you and all men might honor and worship Him as Father.

"Thy kingdom come, thy will be done, on earth as in heaven." As you come alive to His greatness and love begin seeking His will. Again do not rush in with your will, with your desires and requests. It may be that in the moment you think you have something that you want God to do, He has something infinitely more important that He wants you to do. His will is so much greater than our will, so much wider, so much more loving. His will takes in both your life and the life of the whole world. It is so much broader and stronger. It is by His will that the worlds were created. His will sustains history and only what He wills will finally survive. Learn to love His will, to seek it every day. Let the prayer, "Thy will be done," become the very core of your being. Around this prayer organize your life. Learn to quiet yourself again and again before the will of God.

"Give us today our daily bread. Forgive us the wrong we have done, as we have forgiven those who have wronged us. And do

not bring us to the test, but save us from the evil one." Now, having hallowed God's name, having opened yourself to His will, bring to Him your needs. Do this, not because God does not know your needs without your mentioning them, but simply because God wants to respond to you in a personal way. He loves you and wants to relate to you as a living personality, not as though you were some dumb animal. Your will, your faith, your love, and your initiative are important to Him. He takes them into account in His care of the world. So do not hesitate asking Him for your needs, so long as you honor Him and seek His will.

Ask Him to supply your *present* physical needs. Ask Him for bread, for shelter. Seek God's help in the practical affairs of your daily life. Ask Him for help in overcoming the failures of the *past*. Ask Him for forgiveness. Do not carry the burdens of past misconduct into the present. Ask God to lift from you the curse of guilt, so that your mind and heart can be clear for the future. Remember, however, that if you do not forgive others, God cannot forgive you. Never come to prayer while harboring a grudge against someone else. Ask God for help in facing the *future* victoriously. Ask Him for deliverance from evil. Do not begin a day without asking God's assistance in overcoming the trials and temptations of that day.

Before leaving the "Lord's Prayer," it should be noted that a footnote has been attached to it (verses 14 and 15). This footnote singles out one phrase for special comment and emphasis: "Forgive us our debts, as we also have forgiven our debtors." That this phrase should receive special attention suggests both how important it is and yet how easy it might be to overlook it. Most of us are all too unaware of the repercussions our attitudes toward others have on our relation to God. We often come to God in a careless way, expecting a gracious reception, no matter how badly we have dealt with others. This concept of "cheap grace," as Dietrich Bonhoeffer called it, is sharply challenged by the teachings of Jesus.

On one occasion He told of a servant whose king forgave him an enormous debt of ten million dollars (Matthew 18:23 ff.). No sooner was this servant set free than he went and enslaved a man who owed him just twenty dollars. When the king heard about it, he was angry and had this servant thrown into prison. To act in this way is to destroy the fabric of God's purpose in forgiveness. Mercy is shown to us that we might in turn show mercy. God frees us to make us free for love and service. If in our freedom we turn and destroy others, we only show how totally we have misunderstood the character of God.

Therefore, away with grudges and hard feelings! "For if you forgive men their trespasses, your heavenly Father also will forgive you; but if you do not forgive men their trespasses, neither will your Father forgive your trespasses."

b. *Property* (Matthew 6:19-34)

If, as we said above, many people in our time have a thoughtless and unquestioning attitude toward prayer, this is even more the case when it comes to property. Concerning possessions the attitude by and large seems to be, "The more, the better." The love of money, far from being thought of as the "root of all evil," is accorded the status of a virtue. Men of wealth are admired and emu- lated. When they apply for membership in our churches they are welcomed with few questions asked. Jesus said it would be hard for rich men to enter the kingdom of God (Matthew 19:23, 24). It has become easy for them to enter the ranks of the church. The result is that inside our churches, no less than outside, we find people practicing what Jesus describes as a "Gentile" or "heathen- ish" economic life (6:32).

There is a great need that we ask our- selves, as we did with regard to prayer: Lord, teach us!

We have already commented on the con- text and form of Jesus' words in Matthew 6:19-34, but it may be helpful to repeat those comments, for both the setting of the teaching here and the manner of it are instructive in themselves. So far as the *context* is concerned the important point is that Jesus deals with the question of property in conjunction with prayer and piety. This already indicates a point of view toward this question different from that which prevails in our time. The property question is not simply a legal or social matter. How we relate to our possessions has psychological and spiritual consequences. It affects our relation to God.

So far as the *form* of the teaching is concerned, it is worth observing again that Jesus continues to address us with sharp commands. Here, as heretofore, He wants to engage our will. In addition to the commands, however, another form of teaching is introduced. A number of statements and sayings in this section may be classified as proverbial or wisdom-type sayings. The point of wisdom sayings is not to challenge the will but to awaken insight. These sayings stimulate our imagination and lead us to new levels of understanding. The expansion of this kind of teaching right at this point in the Sermon implies that in our relation to property we need more than commandments. We need comprehension. We need a grasp of what is at stake. As such this section of teaching calls us not only to decision but to meditation and reflection as well.

The teachings here may be summarized as follows:

There are two commands (the second one repeated three times), each followed by several wisdom sayings, and then a third command which summarizes the whole matter.

We may diagram the passage this way:

First Command: "Do not lay up for yourselves treasures on earth . . . lay up for yourselves treasures in heaven" (verse 19).

79

Insights: 1. "Where your wealth is, there will your heart be also" (verse 21).

2. "The lamp of the body is the eye. If your eyes are sound, you will have light for your whole body" (verses 22, 23).

3. "No man can serve two masters" (verse 24).

Second Command: "Therefore I tell you, do not be anxious about your life" (verses 25, 31, 34).

Insights: 1. "Is not life more than food" (verse 25)?

2. "And which of you by being anxious can add one cubit to his span of life" (verse 27)?

3. "Look at the birds . . . the lilies. . . . Are you not of more value? . . . Your heavenly Father knows that you need them all" (verses 26, 28, 32).

4. "Each day has troubles enough of its own" (verse 34).

Summary Command: "But seek first his kingdom and his righteousness, and all these things shall be yours as well" (verse 33).

Perhaps no teachings of Jesus strike a modern reader with more astonishment and perplexity than these. At first glance they seem to sound an almost idyllic note, as though meant for some far-off island untouched by the rush of modern life. What meaning can they have for us who must live in a technologically complex world and daily face economic problems undreamed of by those of an earlier generation? Let us look more closely at each of the commands with this question in mind.

The First Command: "Do not lay up for yourselves treasures on earth . . . but lay up for yourselves treasures in heaven" (6:19, 20).

If any words could be said to express the heart of Jesus' concern regarding property and wealth, it would be these. He repeats them, or words like them, almost every time He is reported to have spoken on this subject. (See below.) What is their meaning?

The *first part* of this double command ("Do not lay up for yourselves treasures on earth") obviously contradicts a widely accepted and cherished notion in our society, the notion that it is honorable to accumulate personal wealth. Few ideas are more deeply entrenched in the life of our Western societies than this one, that a man has a right to amass private properties and do with them as he pleases.

When children grab from one another and pout, "This is mine," their parents try to teach them to share; but when these same children grow up and earn their tens of thousands of dollars, grabbing it for themselves and saying in effect, "This is mine," we admire them for being enterprising citizens. It is this unchallenged possessiveness which has led to the injustices which all too often accompany and corrupt Western capitalism.

Jesus, however, teaches us differently. The

resources of this earth, His words imply, have not been given to any man to lay up for himself, no matter how legitimate the means by which he might have obtained them. Jesus wants His disciples to put an end to this kind of selfish accumulation.

If the goal of our economic pursuits is not that of laying up wealth for ourselves on earth, what then is it to be? "But lay up for yourselves treasures in heaven." The alternative to storing up treasures for ourselves on earth is to lay them up in heaven. But how does one do that? Where is this heavenly bank account and how does one go about depositing treasures there?

The Gospels suggest that the rather strange-sounding words, "treasure in heaven," were often on the lips of Jesus. On several occasions the context makes it clear just what He meant. To the rich young ruler, for example, Jesus said, "Sell all that you have and *distribute to the poor,*" and then, He added, "you will have treasure in heaven" (Luke 18:22). On another occasion, when speaking to all the disciples on this same subject, Jesus said, "Fear not, little flock. . . . Sell your possessions, and *give alms;* provide yourselves with purses that do not grow old, with a treasure in the heavens that does not fail" (Luke 12:32 ff.). From these and other sayings in the Gospels it is clear that by His summons to lay up treasure in heaven, Jesus meant: Give alms, distribute to the poor. The rich man whose only thought was to pull down his barns and build bigger ones is described as "not rich toward God" (Luke 12:21). The way to increase our spiritual bank account is by decreasing our material accounts through generosity toward those in need.

In short: The command against accumulating wealth for ourselves on earth and the summons to lay it up instead in heaven is simply Jesus' way of asking us to take a more unselfish and loving attitude toward our wealth. It is His way of challenging the haves to share with the have-nots. He does not tell us *how* this should be done. He does not specify any particular economic or social system. He leaves the implementation of this command to our own imagination. As to the fundamental issue involved, however, He allows us no alternative. Like Israel's prophets before Him Jesus speaks decisively and passionately for economic sharing and justice. He calls His disciples to be a community marked by generosity.

Significantly, it is this very point that Jesus sought to illustrate in one of His few parables devoted to the problem of wealth, the story of the dishonest steward (Luke 16:1-9). In that parable the steward, realizing that he is about to lose his job, goes to his master's debtors and vastly reduces the amounts they owe, distributing in effect large sums of his master's wealth. Jesus summarizes the point of this story in these words: "I tell you, make friends for yourselves by means of unrighteous mammon, so that when it fails they may receive you into the eternal habitations" (Luke 16:9). By distributing to those who need it in this life, Jesus tells us, we create bonds of friendship which will benefit us in the life to come.

All this is further emphasized by Jesus in the three wisdom sayings which are attached to this opening command. "Where your wealth is, there will your heart be also." Wealth and property have a peculiar way of capturing our affections. Where is your heart? Is it bound up in the accumulation of money and things? Or is it concerned for the needs of others?

"The eye is the lamp of the body. . . . If your eye is not sound your whole body will be full of darkness." In speaking of a diseased eye that can fill our whole body with darkness, Jesus very likely means covetousness, "the lust of the eye." As you look around, do you have such a covetous eye, lusting for the things others possess? Or is your eye sound, focused on God and His kingdom?

"You cannot serve God and mammon." What is really mastering your life? The will of God, or the desire for more money, bigger barns, more land, larger houses, more and more things? So long as we are in the grip of greed, so long as we are serving mammon, we *cannot* serve His cause or know the reality of God, for God wills justice and sharing.

The Second Command: "Therefore I bid you put away anxious thoughts about food and drink to keep you alive, and clothes to cover your body" (Matthew 6:25, NEB).

If, as we have seen, the first command discussed above contains some rather puzzling terminology, the same could not be said about this second one. Every adult knows exactly what Jesus is talking about when He speaks of "anxious thoughts about food and drink . . . and clothes to cover your body." Our anxieties, it seems, have kept pace with the rapid development in modern times of a higher and more complex standard of life. The more we have, the more we worry; and the more we worry, the more desperately we try to secure ourselves against the possible losses and disasters of an unknown future. One result has been the rise of a multi-billion-dollar insurance industry covering every conceivable type of potential problem or difficulty. In this way modern men have tried to still their anxious thought about material needs.

Jesus, however, bids us put away anxious thoughts altogether. His antidote for the poison of worry is stated in the glowing words about faith in God which immediately follow this command. In few other passages in the Gospels do we find Jesus speaking so imaginatively of God's love as here. His words reflect pain and astonishment at our inability to see what He saw all around Him: signs of the marvelously creative care that God has lavished on the world. The lilies and grasses of the field and the birds of the air were living witnesses to Him of the love of God. It is not that He closed His eyes to the unpleasant side of nature. We know from His other sayings that He was fully aware of the suffering and evil that exist in the world. But in the midst of these He saw, with prophetic clarity, the handiwork of God. It is He who taught us, in the face of all that is unknown and oftentimes perplexing about the world to say, "Father," "Our Father." Implied here is the truth that only as we are liberated from worry and anxiety by such a faith in a loving Father God will we be able to overcome the tyranny of greed and become the generous people He wants us to be.

The Third Command: "But seek first his kingdom and his righteousness, and all these things shall be yours as well."

This third command provides a provocative summary and conclusion to Jesus' teaching on property and wealth. Throughout this section Jesus seeks to initiate a revolution in our thinking about "things." Our human tendency is first to worry about our own individual life and its needs and only in the second place to give our attention to others. Jesus wants just the opposite. He wants us first of all, and above everything else, to seek that righteous order, that loving community which He spoke of as the kingdom of God. If we seek that kingdom first, Jesus promises, everything else we really need will be supplied as well.

This is an astonishing promise and we might justifiably ask how in practical experience Jesus foresaw it actually working out. There are some clues as to His thinking on this matter in a memorable exchange between His disciples and Himself on the occasion of the departure of the rich ruler referred to above (Mark 10:23-30; Matthew 19:23-29; Luke 18:24-30). Sadly watching him go, Jesus commented, in the hearing of His disciples, that it would be harder for a rich man to enter the kingdom of God than for a camel to go through the eye of a needle. Astonished, His disciples exclaimed: "Who then can be saved?" Jesus assured them that with the help of God all things are possible. Even a rich man with God's help can break free from the stranglehold of wealth.

It was then that Peter blurted out the question that all the disciples must have had, and which we in a sense are asking at this point of our discussion: "Lo, we have left everything and followed you. What then shall we have" (Matthew 19:27)? Those first disciples were examples of men who sought first God's kingdom and its righteousness. But what was to happen to them? How would their needs be supplied?

In His answer Jesus painted a picture of a new society. "Truly, I say to you, there is no one who has left house or brothers or sisters or mother or father or children or lands, for my sake and for the gospel, who will not receive a hundredfold now in this time, houses and brothers and sisters and mothers and children and lands, with persecutions, and in the age to come eternal life" (Mark 10:29, 30). In these words we can sense Jesus' expectation that out of His work a movement would arise, a people who would live together in the spirit of a close and loving family. In the context of this community the man who left all to follow Jesus would find a new sphere of economic and social support. The man who may have had to leave behind his house in order to join this movement would find houses a hundredfold as the doors of all Christian families are now open to him. He who left mother or father or sisters and brothers would find a new comradeship as deep as the ties of blood with all who follow Christ. Though buffeted by persecutions and trials of various kinds the needs of the disciples will be met, these words imply, *by a loving God working through a generous people.* That is Jesus' vision of economic life among His disciples.

In Luke's description of the first Christian community in Acts 2:43-47 and 4:32-37, as well as in the writings of Paul and the history of the church, we can find numerous illustrations of the outworking of this teaching. Those who have taken Jesus' counsels on economic life seriously have found them far from idyllic or impractical. They are part of His total vision of life as God meant it to be, lived in harmony and love and in reverence for God and His will.

In summary: Wherever Christian disciples gather they will reveal in their life together a new spirit in the way they hold their property in relation to God and the needs of their fellowmen. Because they no longer worship mammon, but are devoted to God, they will be set free to live without anxiety, sharing their possessions with one another and those in need everywhere. The Christian fellowship will be known for its generosity, for its spirit of unselfishness and sharing.

The following "Property Attitudes Checklist" is intended to assist you in reviewing the teachings we have just discussed and to personalize them for your own life.

PROPERTY ATTITUDES CHECKLIST
(Based on the teaching of Jesus found in Matthew 6:19-34)

Put a check mark in the blank space in front of each statement after you are sure you understand it and can fully subscribe to it.

1. —— *I have firmly decided to take an unselfish and detached attitude toward my possessions and share them with those in need* (6:19, 20). In order to carry out this decision in a faithful way:

2. —— I have undertaken an examination of my attitudes toward the things I *currently* possess to discover to what extent I consider them "mine" and therefore am personally bound up with them. On the basis of this self-examination I can say that my property is not my "treasure" (6:21).

3. —— I have also examined my attitude toward things I do not possess, to discover to what extent my life is darkened by the evil eye of covetousness. In the light of this I can also

say I am free from the desire for other people's things (6:22, 23).

4. —— I have asked myself whether I am motivated by the quest for money rather than by the service of God's will, and I do not hesitate saying that God rather than money has first place in my life (6:24).

5. —— *I have firmly decided to put away anxious thoughts about my physical needs* (6:25). In order to carry out this decision in a faithful way:

6. —— I have sought to deepen my awareness of how much more meaning life has than simply food, clothing, or shelter (6:25).

7. —— I have considered how little control I have over my material existence and hence how futile it is to worry (6:27).

8. —— Most important, I have thought about the reality of God's love until I truly do believe that the "Father" knows what I need and will care for me in the same way He cares for the lesser parts of His creation (6:26, 28-32).

9. —— I have also come to understand the wisdom of the maxim: Each day has troubles enough of its own (6:34).

10. —— In summary: *I have decided to put first in my life God's kingdom and all that entails by way of a just, loving, and righteous life with others, trusting that as I do so everything else nec-*

essary for my livelihood will be provided (6:33).

This section of our study, as the previous one, calls us into covenant. The following is an attempt to summarize the teachings of chapter 6 in the form of an agreement encompassing our relation to God.

A COVENANT FOR CHRISTIAN DISCIPLES
Concerning Our Life with God
Based on Matthew 6

1. *Concerning Piety:* I will carefully guard against turning my transactions with God into a self-exalting display before men, by hiding my piety from the eyes of men and seeking to grow in my awareness of, and accountability before God (6:1-6, 16-18).

2. *Concerning Prayer:* Trusting that God knows what I need, I will reject the anxious practice of prayer prevalent among the "Gentiles," whereby they suppose that God hears them because of their many words, and seek instead to understand and practice the pattern of prayer set forth in the Lord's Prayer (6:7-15).

3. *Concerning Property:* Believing that God knows and values me and having confidence that He will supply everything I really need by way of food, clothing, and shelter as I seek His will and His way, I will give up anxious thoughts about the material side of life, take a detached attitude toward my properties, and share them generously with my fellow disciples and men in need everywhere (6:19-34).

Concluding Admonitions and Warnings

(Matthew 7)

A. Introduction

If we pause at this point in our study, as we should, and look back on the way of life set before us in Matthew, chapters 5 and 6, taking the whole of it in at a glance, we will become keenly aware of the breadth and intensity of its challenge. Here in these chapters we catch a glimpse of a new kind of person (5:3-16), one marked by humility, openness, trust toward God, and zeal for the right, bearing the fruits of mercy, purity, peace, and courage in the face of suffering. Here too is a vision of social life (5:17-48) uncorrupted by anger and recrimination, untainted by sexual lust and marital infidelity, where men speak the truth to one another from the heart, and love reigns so fully that even evil men cannot shatter it with their thoughtless deeds and persecutions. And here too is profound instruction concerning the possibilities of a faith in God (chapter 6), unsullied by hypocritical religious conventionalities, kept alive by prayer that is actively engaged with the reality of a loving God, and characterized by a loyalty so great that even the tyranny of property is broken and we are set free to become instruments of justice and sharing.

Again and again it has been asked by those who have sensed something of the radical challenge of the Sermon: Is it real? Is it meant for this world? Does Jesus intend that we should realize this vision now? Or is it, as one contemporary theologian has said, an "impossible possibility"? Is it a possibility, but one that we cannot hope to realize in a world as deeply corrupted as ours is by evil powers?

The final chapter of the Sermon on the Mount leaves us in no doubt as to how we are to answer these questions. The whole of chapter 7 is devoted to a series of problems having to do with the realization of the vision set before us in the previous two chapters. Few sections of Jesus' teaching reveal as clearly as this one His grasp of human realities and His clarity concerning the struggles His disciples would have to engage in as they sought to follow His way. Whatever else may be said of Jesus, it cannot be maintained that He was an idealist, moving in a realm detached from the world of ordinary men. He knew what was in the heart of men and He knew what was ahead for His disciples.

He saw the potential pitfalls. He saw the corruption that would descend even upon His own movement. Unlike so many starry-eyed reformers, He had no fantasy as to the character or strength of His followers. He knew there would be among them the faithful and the unfaithful, the true and the false, the weak and the strong. He knew that the way He walked and taught was not easy and that relatively few would stay with it to the end. He knew the subtle bypaths that would divert some of the most zealous of His followers from reaching their goal.

It is of these things that Jesus speaks in this final chapter. His teachings here are worthy of the most careful study by those who would follow in this way to a successful conclusion.

Eight distinct units of teaching make up the content of this chapter. Each unit touches upon a unique and vital issue.

The first four teaching units in verses 1-12 may be characterized as *admonitions*. In an admonition someone who loves us and has our welfare at stake solemnly exhorts us with reference to some real or potential problem in our lives. The danger to which an admonition is addressed is typically a danger *within us*.

The final four teaching paragraphs of this chapter in verses 13-27 may be termed *warnings*. A warning is at the same time less personal and more urgent than an admonition. The danger to which a warning is addressed is *more external*. In this case it has to do with the disastrous loss of faith that can overtake us through the influence of compromised and compromising people around us.

B. Study

Four Admonitions (Matthew 7:1-12)

We will turn our attention first of all to the admonitions in 7:1-12. Check out the validity of the suggestion that the four admonitions here look back on the teaching already given and answer the following questions:

1. How shall I use this teaching in relation to fellow disciples? (7:1-5)

2. How shall I use this teaching in relation to those outside the community of disciples? (7:6)

3. How can I ever attain to the life indicated by this teaching? (7:7-11)

4. How should I conduct myself in situations not covered by this teaching? (7:12)

If these are the questions presupposed by the four admonitions, how are they answered? Study each admonition with the questions suggested above in mind. Summarize the answer given by each admonition in your own words. Compare your summary with the following:

Answer to Question One: Never take a condemning attitude toward anyone. Use this teaching first and foremost as a criticism of your own life. Only when you have dealt with your faults will you see clearly enough to help your brother overcome his.

Answer to Question Two: In bringing this teaching to the world be alert to a type of person who mocks at truth. Do not carelessly press these "pearls" of the kingdom upon such men. It will only have bad consequences.

Answer to Question Three: You can find power to live as Jesus taught through thoughtful ("seeking"), earnest ("knocking") prayer, spurred on by the hope and the confidence that God is good and will give us every good thing we need.

Answer to Question Four: In summary let this be your guide in every situation: Consider how you would like others to treat you; then treat others that same way.

The following comments on each admonition may assist you in further understanding their intent and implications.

The First Admonition (7:1-5)

An important clue to the problem area touched on by this opening admonition is the thrice repeated word "brother." Jesus addresses Himself in this initial admonition to a problem that frequently arises among fellow disciples. He pinpoints a difficulty often found in the relationships of people who covenant together in pursuit of lofty goals.

The righteous zeal of such people easily turns to self-righteousness. Their high sense of responsibility before God can lead to a suffocating criticism of one another.

Jesus warns against this. Some have taken His warning as a rejection of any and every form of mutual admonition or criticism. His words, "Judge not . . ." have sometimes been interpreted as meaning: "Your brother's conduct is none of your business. Leave him alone." Such a reading of this passage, how-

ever, misses the point of the last and cul-
minating sentence of this paragraph: "Then
you will see clearly to take the speck out of
your brother's eye" (7:5). Jesus' words here
are not meant to prohibit mutual concern but
to insure that this concern is expressed in such
a way that it achieves a redemptive purpose.
He wants to make sure that in admonishing
one another we "see clearly."

This is in accord with Jesus' instructions as
stated elsewhere in His teaching. In Matthew
18:15, for example, in the context of a passage
of great importance for understanding His
thinking about the church, He says, "If your
brother sins against you, go and tell him his
fault, between you and him alone. If he lis-
tens to you, you have gained your brother."
Again in Luke 17:3 He is reported to have
said, "Take heed to yourselves; if your brother
sins, rebuke him, and if he repents, forgive
him." The Apostle Paul indicates in Galatians
6:1, 2 that this practice of brotherly admonition was of vital importance in the early
church. It could be spoken of as fulfilling the
"law of Christ." "Brethren, if a man is over-
taken in any trespass, you who are spiritual
should restore him in a spirit of gentleness.
Look to yourself, lest you too be tempted.
Bear one another's burdens, and so fulfill the
law of Christ."

Far, then, from depreciating the help that
disciples owe one another, Jesus encourages
it, but warns, in this first admonition, against

its perversion. In exercising spiritual and moral responsibility for one another Jesus wants us to guard against judging. We must refrain from condemning one another. We must not take a superior attitude. We must not seek to hurt or punish. We must not wield the words of Jesus like a whip.

Instead, prior to any attempt to bring these teachings to bear upon the life of another, the person bringing the admonition must examine himself.

It is a well-known human trait to be very much alive to the faults of others while blind to our own. Psychologists speak of this as projection. We project onto others the problems and faults we are fighting within ourselves. Jesus wants us to be aware of this tendency and fight against it. He does not want us even to look at the fault of another, much less think about it, or seek to correct it, until we have first examined ourselves.

Only when we have undergone repentance ourselves will we be able to lead others in repentance. Only when we have faced up to anger in our own lives, and in pain and sorrow rooted it out, will we have the wisdom and compassion to help another through the struggle against anger. Only if we have allowed ourselves to see to what extent we are corrupted by lust, and have repented of it, are we in a position to help another to victory in this troublesome area. And so it is with all the other issues touched on by Jesus in

His teachings. We cannot apply these teachings responsibly and helpfully to our fellow disciples until our own lives have been cleansed.

But once that has happened, then we are able and not only able, but obligated to help a struggling brother. The image that Jesus uses of picking a speck from an eye implies delicacy. It implies gentleness and finesse. In order to pick out a speck from an eye you do not push roughly in with any utensil that may be at hand. The whole eye might be lost! When we have been deeply humbled through repentance in the presence of Jesus and His teaching, we will cease barging in upon our brother with the cudgels of crude condemnation. We will go to him in humility and gentleness, fully aware of our own faults, and knowing that in the future we will very likely need this same brother to help us.

This counsel is badly needed and should be thoroughly pondered by every convert. When becoming aware of the fault of another, it is so easy to do two things: (1) glory in it; (2) gossip about it. We glory in it, because his fall accents our standing. We gossip about it to gain status with others. Both of these human tendencies must cease among those who would really be faithful to Christ. Instead of looking at the brother's fault, examine your own. Set a strict guard against gossip. Only when you are spiritually ready, go to the erring brother alone, and in gentleness and love seek to win him away from his fault. If he will not listen, Matthew 18:15 ff. suggests some further steps that may be necessary.

The Second Admonition (Matthew 7:6)

If Jesus in the first admonition addressed Himself to a problem between brothers, it is obvious that here in this second admonition the focus has shifted. It is not brothers about whom we read in Matthew 7:6, but "dogs" and "swine." Among the Jewish people these two terms, "dogs" and "swine," stood for all that is unclean and shameful. "Skunks" and "rats" we might say today.

Jesus, as we said above, was a realist. His lofty vision of what men might be with the help of God did not blind Him to the reality of what men are. He foresaw that His disciples would not only have to contend with problems among one another within the circle of disciples, but they would also have to face difficult issues in their relations with "dogs" and "swine." These are men and women who have lost all moral and spiritual discretion. Having corrupted themselves they have no qualms against corrupting others. Their belly is their god, Paul once wrote of them, and they mock at truth (Philippians 3:19).

At issue in this second admonition is the relation of the disciple to such people. The "pearls" mentioned here are without doubt the teachings which we have been studying. In Matthew 13:45 f. Jesus likened the kingdom to a pearl of great price. The question presupposed then by this admonition has to do with our use of Jesus' teachings in relation to hostile outsiders. What role shall these "pearls" of wisdom and insight play in my relations with evil men outside the community of disciples?

The answer suggested by this brief admonition is one of caution. It is dangerous to try to bring these teachings to bear upon a life that has no openness for them. As a missionary strategy it is destined to cause more harm than good. The economic teaching of Jesus, for example, will only look like fanaticism to those whose hearts are bent on accumulation. The impure man is enraged by what he considers the laughable Puritanism of Jesus' counsels on sex. Any attempt to bring this teaching to bear upon his life will only arouse a storm of mockery. To the godless man, prayer as taught by Jesus is a form of self-deception. Do not take these teachings, Jesus admonishes, and expose them to those who have no openness for them.

This does not mean, of course, that we should have no relations with such men. This does not mean the end of any kind of responsibility. In the final pages of Matthew's Gospel we read of a commission given by Jesus to His apostles to go forth and make disciples of all nations (Matthew 28:19). Jesus came to seek and to save the lost, and who are more lost than just those "dogs" and "swine" about whom He speaks here. However, these will not be won by thrusting upon them the insights of the Sermon on the Mount.

101

The Sermon on the Mount, as has been repeatedly suggested, is for disciples. It is for those who have already opened their lives to Jesus and to the will of God revealed in Him. Condemning the world in the light of the Sermon on the Mount will not draw it to Jesus Christ. It will only arouse anger and bring the teachings into disrepute.

Under no circumstances, then, should we admonish hostile outsiders on the basis of these teachings. Only when we have thoroughly examined and purged our own lives of the faults involved are we in a position to help anyone else along this way, and even then the only ones who might be helped are those who want to be helped. If we want to win the world to the Christ of the Mount, let us live the way He taught. Let us dwell on these words of Jesus until they become such a part of our lives that His way will be natural to us. Then the world will see what it means to be a Christian. Not our words thrust upon them, but our lives freely and spontaneously lived in their midst will bear the message. (See also the discussion of Matthew 5:13, 14 above.)

The Third Admonition (7:7-11)

At this point in the Sermon on the Mount it would seem we have a repetition of teaching given earlier. The subject of this admonition is prayer. This subject was already discussed in chapter 6. There, however, prayer was dealt with against the larger background of anxiety about material needs and in the context of our relation to God and His kingdom. Here only one dimension of prayer is emphasized, prayer as a sure way of obtaining certain "good things" (verse 11) that we most desperately need.

"Ask, and it will be given you;
    Seek, and you will find;
        Knock, and it will be opened to you.
    For every one who asks receives,
        and he who seeks finds;
            and to him who knocks,
                it will be opened."

At first glance it might seem that this teaching about prayer contradicts the teaching given earlier. In chapter 6 Jesus emphasized the fact that God knows our needs even before we ask Him, and consequently we do not need to babble endlessly about them. Here He stresses that there is a clear and definite link between our asking, seeking, and knocking and what we receive.

The teaching on prayer here in chapter 7, however, presupposes a very different kind of problem from that in chapter 6. The problem is not stated for us, but it should be obvious to anyone who has participated in the study so far. For we only need to ask ourselves, What problem do *we* feel at this juncture of our study? Are we not painfully aware by this time of our personal inadequacies? How much in us must change in the light of all that Jesus says to us in the Sermon on the Mount! What a revolution His words require! The question presupposed by this third admonition is the one uttered by the Apostle Paul at the conclusion of his passionate self-examination in Romans 7: "Wretched man that I am! Who will deliver me from this body of death" (Romans 7:24)? Jesus is not speaking here, as in chapter 6, to the Gentiles' anxiety about *physical needs,* but to the disciple's recognition of *spiritual need.* To those who are asking, "How can I ever hope to attain to the life described by Jesus in the Sermon on the Mount?" He is saying, "Ask, seek, knock!" There are resources available.

The point at stake here is pinpointed by Luke's version of this same teaching. In Luke the concluding line of teaching reads, "How much more will the heavenly Father give the *Holy Spirit* to those who ask him" (Luke 11:13)! The "good things" mentioned by Matthew are interpreted in Luke's version as the Holy Spirit. From beginning to end Jesus presupposes in His life and teaching that the renewal of mankind and the birth of a new social order will require more than moral imperatives, more than strenuous effort on man's part. His own ministry began with the descent of the Holy Spirit upon Him (Mark 1:10). His coming was prophesied by John as the coming of One who would baptize, not with water, but with the Spirit (Mark 1:8). And among the last words of Jesus to His disciples were words of promise as to the coming of the Spirit upon them (Acts 1:8). Jesus knew that men needed not only a new way, but a new experience of personal life from God.

Unlike physical gifts, however, this "life"

cannot be given where it is not received. It cannot be imparted where it is not wanted. I can feed my enemy. I can give him bread. But I cannot give him a sense of my good will. I cannot impart to him a sense of my love. No matter how much I adore the girl of my affections, no matter how many gifts I give her, I cannot give her what I most want to share—myself—until she opens herself to me. The spirit of a man cannot force its way upon another. And even when once shared, the least gesture of rejection is enough to send it away.

These are poor analogies to the deepest mystery of God sharing His Spirit with us. But they are intended to help us see why it is so important in spiritual matters that we ask, that we seek and knock. When we do so, Jesus promises, God will most certainly give us His Holy Spirit. *Everyone* who seeks, Jesus promises, will find God. God is ready and waiting to share of Himself. He is waiting to fill us with His Spirit and empower us to live in the new way to which He calls us.

Let no disciple, then, proceed in the Christian way without asking for the Holy Spirit. It is the privilege of every Christian to know the daily companionship of the Holy Spirit. It is the privilege of every Christian to know the daily companionship of Jesus. The Holy Spirit is nothing else but the spiritual presence of Jesus and of God. We are not talking about theological fine points regarding the Trinity. We are talking about an experience whereby we know that the God and Father of Jesus Christ is present with us in and through His Spirit. "Lo, I am with you always," Jesus promised His disciples just before ascending into heaven (Matthew 28:20). "Wherever two or three of you gather in my name, I am in your midst" (Matthew 18:20). Ask and you will experience Jesus as a helping presence. Seek and God's Holy Spirit will lead you. Paul could say, summarizing the whole mystery of the Christian life: "Anyone who does not have the Spirit of Christ does not belong to him . . . for all who are led by the Spirit of God are sons of God" (Romans 8:9, 14). The Christian life is not just a matter of insights and commands but of life in fellowship with the Spirit of God.

Pray, then, to God for His Spirit, if you have not done so already. Open your heart to a living experience.

The Fourth Admonition (7:12)

This series of admonitions closes with a maxim found in its negative formulation among various peoples of the world. The Stoics before Christ had a saying: "Do not to another what you do not wish to happen to yourself." And Confucius was reported to have said, "Do not to others what you would not wish done to yourself." It is not without significance that Jesus revised this piece of well-known moral advice in a positive way: "Whatever you wish that men would do to you, do so to them." With this seemingly simple innovation He gave to this ancient saying a new and more effective role in our struggle to over-come our deep-seated selfishness.

But before we pursue this line of thinking further, we should pause to consider what question, or what need is spoken to by this brief concluding admonition. Again if we con-sult our feelings, we will become aware of a dilemma which the Sermon on the Mount pos-es for us, especially as we contemplate leaving it to take up the tasks of our modern life. That dilemma is simply that the Sermon is all too brief. While it touches on the major categories of life experience and speaks to many really fundamental problems, there are issues and questions confronting us every day not mentioned at all. In comparison with other documents, ancient or modern, setting forth a comprehensive way of life it is astonish-ingly terse and unelaborated. How shall I act, what attitude shall I take, how shall I think in relation to all those issues and situations not specifically dealt with by the teachings of this Sermon? These are the questions that we are left with as we come to the close of our study, and to which this final admonition speaks.

The answer, which we have come to refer to as the "Golden Rule," implies that the Ser-mon on the Mount is indeed an incomplete document. It was not intended to be other-wise. For what is lacking in the Sermon, the words of this "Rule" suggest, is to be made up, in part at least, by our own moral imagina-tion and creativity. This "Rule," in fact, is not so much a rule at all, but a stimulant, prodding us to a moral maturity beyond rules.

It is as if Jesus were saying: You do not need advice from Me for every decision. You do not need My authoritative guidance for every problem. Just look within and you will find the secret of the law and the prophets. How do you want people to treat you? Treat others that same way. "Whatever you wish that men would do to you, do so to them, for this is the law and the prophets."

It is sometimes thought that the "Golden Rule" estimates our moral capabilities too highly. To say this, however, is to overlook the fact that this "Rule" takes as its starting point, not our moral strength, but a human condition that may be described as the essence of sinfulness: our self-centeredness. It quietly assumes that we are selfish. The unique power of this "Rule" depends in fact upon the force of this all too prevalent human weakness. For it asks us to put this "self-love" to work for others. It summons us to project out into our interpersonal relations the same sensitivity which is so powerfully at work when looking after our own interests. It seeks to turn the tables on our selfishness by enlisting it in the service of love.

In this sense the practice of this "Rule" can assist us in overcoming our narrow personal attitudes and set us in motion toward a more outgoing, humane, and loving life, which indeed is all that the law and prophets are about.

FOUR CLOSING WARNINGS
Based on Matthew 7:13-27

The four warnings which stand at the
close of the Sermon on the Mount focus on
some of the major sources of confusion and
compromise which were to plague the Christian
movement from the very beginning and are
still at work in the church today. Admonitions
are addressed to the mind and will. Warnings
speak to the emotions as well. As we come to
the close of our study, we must understand,
and not only understand, but *feel* the terrible
dangers that lurk in the shadows.

The dangers against which Jesus warns us
are, of course, not physical dangers. Nor can
we speak of them as spiritual dangers, although a spiritual and psychological dimension
is certainly involved. They are dangers
embodied in the lives of people. They are
dangers that present themselves on two legs.
As such they are subtle. In their subtlety, in
fact, lies their danger. When a building is burn-
ing down, everyone can see what is happening.
But when termites are eating away at the
foundations, we may not know it, and have a
hard time believing anything is wrong until
the whole house comes crashing down. Such
are the dangers of which Jesus speaks here.
Hidden behind a facade of success and seem-
ing stability lurk people whose lives and
influence are pernicious. Only if we tear away
the facade can we see them for what they are.

That is what Jesus is doing in these warnings: Tearing off the facade and exposing the danger that lurks beneath.

Who are these people? What is wrong with them? And how can we escape being numbered with them in their disaster? These are the questions which we should be asking as we approach these final paragraphs of the Sermon on the Mount. Study each warning with these questions in mind.

Summarize the warnings in your own words. Check your summaries against the following:

1. Do not be discouraged by those *outside* the disciple community who seem to have it easy in comparison to yourself.

To win life in its fullest requires the kind of self-denial and discipline suggested by the Sermon on the Mount. Those who drift along with the crowd following every whim and desire will end up in disaster. Life belongs to those who "strive" to enter the narrow door of moral and spiritual transformation (Matthew 7:13, 14; compare Luke 13:23).

Neither be misled by those *inside* the Christian community who appear to be disciples, but do not practice what Jesus taught (7:15-27).

In particular:

2. Beware of *perverse prophetic personalities,* powerful leaders who "dress up" like disciples, but underneath are full of greed, turning the blind trust of the "sheep" to their own gain. The best way to recognize this destructive type is by paying careful attention to the results of their work. Are the fruits

good or bad, in conformity with the teaching of Jesus or against it (7:15-20)?

3. Beware of *lawless miracle workers*, proud of their ability to preach Christian sermons, and perform miraculous deeds, proud of their piety, but careless about "doing" the will of God. Remember, pious words and spectacular wonderworkings are not enough to gain entrance into the kingdom of God. Wicked ways spoil everything else (7:21-23).

4. Beware of *foolish men*, ordinary Christians who try to get along without acting on what Jesus taught. Like men who build a house on surface soil without bothering to dig down to bedrock (compare Luke 6:47-49), their lives lack solid foundation (7:24-27). Only those who lay a foundation below the surface on the hard rock of obedience to the "words" of Jesus will survive the flood tides and judgments of time and eternity.

The following comments may give you some further insight into these warnings. Read them with your own situation in mind. Which of the warnings speaks most directly to your need at this moment in your life? Share your answers to this question with the others with whom you are studying.

The First Warning (Matthew 7:13, 14)

Of the four warnings only the first one identifies a danger from *outside* the disciple community, although this danger too may establish itself on the inside. The following three warnings are directed explicitly to dangers from within. This fact in itself is instructive. It implies that Jesus foresaw the corruption of His movement as primarily an internal problem. History has borne this out. The church has been its own greatest enemy. The world does not so often corrupt the church by onslaughts from without as the church corrupts itself through the presence of compromised people within it.

There is, however, a danger from without, and that is the one suggested by the parable of the two ways, one broad and easy, leading to death, the other narrow and hard leading to life.

It has become abundantly clear through our study of the Sermon on the Mount that the Christian way is a way of discipline. Many of the commandments of Jesus cut directly across the easy instinctual life. Their appeal is to the higher centers of our personalities. They seek to mobilize a part of us that seems to lie dormant too much of the time, and challenge another part that cries for ascendancy. The physical appetites are by no means despised, but they are made subservient to higher ends. The worth of the individual is not denied, but egocentricity is broken by bringing the individual into a new relationship to the sovereignty of God and the claims of others. The whole Sermon on the Mount is directed toward change, sometimes painful change, issuing in a new kind of man in a new kind of society.

Those who respond to this message certainly must experience it at times as a narrow way. The world itself has frequently looked in upon the Christian movement and branded it "too narrow." There lies the danger for the disciple, especially for the disciple first starting out on this way. It seems so hard. It seems so restricted. And there seem to be so few who are really taking this way seriously. From this narrow, hard way, the disciple looks out upon the masses. They seem to walk through life with such ease. All the pleasures of life are theirs: money, sex, fine homes, new and expensive cars, prestige, power. In our time these values of the broad way are more than ever held before our eyes, and it would seem the great majority of people are seeking them. Especially for the new disciple it is a subtle temptation. Why should he give up all these pleasures of the broad way to walk the narrow way of Christ? Why fight against anger? Why fight against lust? Why this constant struggle for truthfulness? Why suffer these wrongs without hitting back? Why this effort to love the unlovely? Why seek to overcome the pride within and glorify God? Why break loose from things, from wealth? Why?

It is the way that leads to life. The other way leads to destruction. The longer you are on this way, the more you will realize this. Opening up out of the narrow way, life will come flowing in. But as for those who pursue the other way, they will gradually lose their grip on life. Death awaits them at the end of their easy pleasure. Jesus said, I came that they may have life, and have it abundantly" (John 10:10). "I am the way, and the truth, and the life" (John 14:6). At this moment in your discipleship, or perhaps a little later on, you may question that. But hold on. Do not envy the ease and prosperity of those on the broad way. Underneath the facade there is a gnawing emptiness. The broad way turns out to be a way of tormenting problems, unfulfilled dreams, and eventual loneliness.

A word of caution must be added, however. We must not mistake petty inconveniences for the narrow way that leads to life. Not every narrow, disciplined way is a life-giving way. Pharisaism might also be called a narrow way. It required great discipline to be a Pharisee, but it was not a life-giving discipline. Puritanism was also a narrow way, but many of the demands that made it seem narrow were inconsequential. Petty human traditions, as we noted earlier, can easily creep into the Christian community and assert themselves as commandments of God. This is tragic. These human traditions overshadow the life-giving disciplines of Christ and turn His way into a travesty of its original design. Against such a narrow way the world recoils with justification.

The Second Warning (Matthew 7:15-20)

The next three warnings, as already suggested, focus on dangers arising from *within* the Christian community. Jesus had no false idealism about His movement. We are told that He knew the hearts of men and did not need to be told what was in a man. He knew that among His followers would be the true and the false. He did not nourish any perfectionist vision about the future of His church. He foresaw clearly the clash and strife that indeed have characterized it down through the ages.

This point needs to be made in our time because it is at odds with the somewhat optimistic attitude that sometimes prevails among Christians because of the ecumenical movement. The ecumenical movement has brought many needed corrections in our mentality as Christians. It has helped us see that many, if not most, of the denominational lines separating Christians from Christians are meaningless. At the same time it has produced a kind of euphoria about the church. It has inspired a hope for a kind of united world Christianity that will never come into existence in our age. It has made it more difficult to face up to the hard reality of the church as it is. Jesus does not want this. He does not want us to whitewash His movement. On the contrary, He wants us to be wide awake to the dangers that lurk right within it.

The first of these dangers He labels, "False Prophets." False prophets are men of strong personality who counterfeit dynamic utterances and inspired leadership. This is not too difficult to do. Such personalities can even present themselves under the guise of meekness and pseudo-love, closely approximating that of the truly Christian personality. Such men can cloak their ravenous nature with sheeplike gentleness. In their subtlety they can be so deceptive that it is almost impossible to distinguish them from the true prophet, the true leader. Only one thing gives them away: their fruits. What is the result of their labors? What kind of community springs up around them? What are the spiritual consequences of their work? Do they and their disciples bear the marks of transformed living suggested by Jesus in His teachings? If not, no matter how powerful their utterances, no matter how vast and prestigious their following, they are false, and need to be avoided.

Jesus does not want us to be gullible, taken in by every leader who arises in His name. "Beware!" Do not be deceived by corrupt prophetic personalities, feeding on the sheep-like innocence of Christian disciples. True, we are to be harmless as doves, but wise as serpents. Everything we have gained from Christ can be lost if we do not stay on the alert against the influence of hypocritical, self-aggrandizing leaders.

The Third Warning (Matthew 7:21-23)

This is one of the most startling and disturbing warnings ever uttered by Jesus. In some respects it parallels the previous warning against false prophets. The men referred to here, however, are more than prophetic leaders. They are men of "many mighty works." They are miracle workers, casting out demons and healing the sick. They are powerful spokesmen for the cause of Christ. They are men of action, performing great services

116

on behalf of the Christian cause, and there are "many" of them! *But most disturbing of all, they are sincere in what they are doing.* Unlike the false prophets who deliberately disguise their ravenous nature and are out to exploit the Christian movement for their own gain, these men are sincerely dedicated to the cause of Jesus. Nevertheless, they are headed for disaster. On the day of judgment they are astonished to hear that Jesus never knew them, never counted them a part of His movement, and wants nothing to do with them. Why? Because they are evildoers, because they do not do the will of "my Father who is in heaven."

This passage lets us see with blinding clarity how much Jesus values obedience and good character above everything else. No mighty works can make up for it. No powerful sermons, no professions of faith, no miraculous healings. The marks of discipleship are first and foremost fruits of character, fruits of *His* Spirit: love, joy, peace, patience, kindness, goodness, faithfulness, gentleness, self-control (Galatians 5:22, 23). If these are not present we do not belong to His movement, no matter how great our organizational achievements, no matter how masterful our sermons, no matter how miraculous our works. Jesus does not want us ever to forget this.

The Fourth Warning (Matthew 7:24-27)

If there were ever any doubts as to whether Jesus meant His teachings in the Sermon on the Mount to be carried out in actual practice, this final warning should certainly be sufficient to destroy them. It is difficult to imagine how Jesus could make the point any stronger. He wants us to act; He wants us to put His teachings into practice and not just passively listen.

The utter simplicity and urgency with which this point is made in this final paragraph of the Sermon implies a very special danger. Jesus must have foreseen that just this passive attitude of "hearing but not doing" would be present among many of His would-be followers. We do not need to look far to discover that He saw rightly.

In our own time there is a pervasive nonchalance among Christians toward the teachings of Jesus. Men call Him Lord, but fail to respect His words as marching orders for the church. One would think that anyone confessing Jesus as Lord and Master would hang on His every word. One would think that he would rather lose everything than disobey a single command. But it is obviously not so.

Jesus says, "Love your enemies," but the vast majority of Christians, with the consent of the churches, do not hesitate to participate in the ever more horrible wars of the various nations. Jesus says, "No anger," "No lust," "No falsehood," "No retaliation," but all too many Christians look upon these teachings as an impossible ideal. He says, "Beware of practicing your piety before men to be seen by them," but the churches often carelessly display such a volume of religiosity that the world chokes. He says, "Do not lay up treasures for yourselves on earth, but lay up treasures in heaven," but we honor those who have accumulated great wealth and enshrine their names on our churches and institutions.

He calls the meek, the poor in spirit, the merciful, the pure in heart, the hungry and thirsty for righteousness, the persecuted in a righteous cause—He calls them blessed. But we keep on blessing the proud, the crafty, and the eminently successful. We raise the cross of Christ as the most prominent symbol of our faith, but do not follow in the steps of the crucified.

Well did Jesus foresee that all this would be so. And over all this cheap hearing and honoring of His words, over all this hypocritical disobedience He pronounces the word, "Foolish!" "Every one who hears these words of mine and dces not do them will be like a foolish man. . . ." There are churches built on sand, and there are churches built on rock. Only time will tell the difference. When the times of testing come, the foolish Christians forsake their faith. Prior to that they were worshiping, they were pious, they were hearing the preaching, Sunday by Sunday, and receiving the sacraments. But that counts for nothing, when there is no obedience.

The wise are those who hear and do. And their house will stand. They may be poor and persecuted. They may have hardly a roof to cover their heads. But their house will stand. It will survive to bless many generations and to salt and light the world. This is the promise of Jesus. And it is backed up by His own life, His death, and His resurrection.

"And when Jesus finished these sayings, the crowds were astonished at his teaching, for he taught them as one who had authority, and not as their scribes."

The following covenant summarizes the content of Matthew, chapter 7, and provides a way of responding to it.

A COVENANT FOR CHRISTIAN DISCIPLES
Concerning Our Practice of Discipleship Based on Matthew 7

1. I will not condemn my fellow disciples, but rather correct my own faults before trying to correct theirs (7:1-5).

2. I will avoid zealously pushing the teachings of Jesus on to others who do not respect them (7:6).

3. I will seek God's help in walking the Christian way (7:7-11).

4. I will practice treating others the way I would like them to treat me (7:12).

5. I will not shrink back from the hardship and discipline involved in following the way of Christ (7:13, 14).

6. I will be on my guard against being led astray by dynamic leaders whose work does not issue in the fruits of Christlike living (7:15-20).

7. I will likewise try never to forget that pious words or mighty works are no substitute for obedience to the will of God (7:21-23).

8. Above all, I will seek to act upon the teachings of Jesus and not be content with simply hearing or understanding them (7:24-27).

Appendix I

QUESTIONS FOR SELF-EXAMINATION
BASED ON MATTHEW 5:3-16

Review your life in the light of these questions.
Take a fearless inventory of its overall direction.
Think concretely. Have pencil and paper in hand
and jot down your thoughts as they come to you.
Ask God to help you see yourself as you really
are.

1. *Blessed are the poor in spirit, for theirs is
the kingdom of heaven.* Do I have exaggerated
notions of myself? Can I recall times and events
when it became painfully clear to me that I was
thinking more highly of myself than I should have?
Do I want to break free from pride and know
myself as I truly am?

2. *Blessed are those who mourn, for they shall
be comforted.* Am I quick to mourn when I do
wrong? Have I confessed my sins, or are there
misdeeds that I am still trying to hide from myself,
from God, and from others? Do I sorrow deeply for
my sins? Or do I make excuses and pass over
them in a quick and superficial manner?

3. *Blessed are the meek, for they shall inherit
the earth.* Do I have a settled faith and trust in
God? Do I love God's will?

4. *Blessed are those who hunger and thirst for
righteousness, for they shall be satisfied.* For what
am I hungering and thirsting? What concerns lie
at the center of my life? Do I have a strong de-

sire to see a more just and loving life among men on this earth?

5. *Blessed are the merciful, for they shall obtain mercy.* Do I forgive those who wrong me? Or do I enjoy holding grudges and complaints against others? Do my compassions go out to those in difficult circumstances? Or do I reject the unlovely and the unlikable?

6. *Blessed are the pure in heart, for they shall see God.* Am I sincere? Are my motives pure? Am I just one thing, outwardly and inwardly? Do my actions spring from my heart and reflect who I know myself to be? Or am I divided and hypocritical?

7. *Blessed are the peacemakers, for they shall be called sons of God.* Where I am present are human relations made smoother, more loving? Or do problems needlessly multiply and petty contentions arise?

8. *Blessed are those who are persecuted for righteousness' sake, for theirs is the kingdom of heaven.* Do I stand up for the right, even when it costs me something? Do I accept joyfully the hardships that come as a consequence of my loyalty to Jesus and His way?

Appendix II

A COVENANT FOR CHRISTIAN DISCIPLES
a. Concerning Our Life with Others
Based on Matthew 5:17-48

In gratitude to God for all that I have come to know and experience through Jesus Christ, and in anticipation of His coming kingdom, I will gladly, with His help, try to uphold the following covenant:

1. *Concerning anger:* I will take a stand not only against murderous deeds, but against angry, destructive thoughts and emotions (5:21, 22), seeking first of all to purge them from my own life and taking care not to become the occasion for anger on the part of another, (a) by confessing and righting my wrongs against my brother *as soon as I become aware of them* (5:23, 24), and (b) by dealing forthrightly with all matters of conflict between myself and another *as soon as they are brought to my attention* (5:25, 26).

2. *Concerning sexual lust:* It is my intention not only to avoid an adulterous act but to stay free from adulterous thoughts (5:27-30), as well as other sexual perversions. On the positive side I will uphold the standard of lifelong marital love and fidelity (5:31, 32).

3. *Concerning false speech:* I will try under all circumstances to speak the truth in love, simply and clearly, and abide by my promises (5:33-37).

4. *Concerning retaliation:* I will guard against taking revenge against anyone who wrongs me or exchanging injury for injury (5:38, 39a). I will seek rather to overcome evil with good (5:39b-42; Romans 12:21).

5. *Concerning enemies:* I will not surrender to to an attitude of hatred toward enemies. Instead, even though I suffer persecution at their hands, I will pray for them and seek their good (5:43-48).

b. Concerning Our Life with God
Based on Matthew 6

1. *Concerning Piety:* I will guard against turning my transactions with God into a self-exalting display for men, by hiding my piety from the eyes of my fellowmen, and by seeking to grow in my awareness of, and accountability before, God (6:1-6, 16-18).

2. *Concerning Prayer:* Trusting that God knows what I need, I will reject the anxious practice of prayer prevalent among the "Gentiles," whereby they suppose that God hears them because of their many words, and seek instead to understand and practice the pattern of prayer set forth in the "Lord's Prayer" (6:7-15).

3. *Concerning Property:* Believing that God knows and values me and having confidence that He will supply everything I really need by way of food, clothing, and shelter as I seek His will and His way, I will give up anxious thoughts about the material side of life, take a detached attitude toward my properties, and share them generously with my fellow disciples and men in need everywhere (6:19-34).

c. Concerning Our Practice of Discipleship Based on Matthew 7

1. I will not condemn my fellow disciples, but rather correct my own faults before trying to correct theirs (7:1-5).

2. I will avoid zealously pushing the teachings of Jesus on to others who do not respect them (7:6).

3. I will seek God's help in walking the Christian way (7:7-11).

4. I will practice treating others the way I would like them to treat me (7:12).

5. I will not shrink back from the hardship and discipline involved in following the way of Christ (7:13, 14).

6. I will be on my guard against being led astray by leaders whose work does not issue in the fruits of Christlike living (7:15-20).

7. I will likewise try never to forget that pious words or mighty works are no substitute for obedience to the will of God (7:21-23).

8. Above all, I will seek to act upon the teachings of Jesus and not be content with simply hearing or understanding them (7:24-27).

Appendix III

BE CAREFUL!
An Admonition Based on Matthew 6:1-6, 16-18

Be on your guard, disciple. Yes, you, precisely you who take your discipleship seriously, watch out! A special danger awaits you, lurking behind every good deed, hiding behind every sacrificial act, concealed within every noble prayer. This danger is so subtle and so hidden that you will not see it unless you look for it most carefully.

The danger is this: Parading your religion to be seen of men, seeking honor and praise from others through good deeds, gaining prestige through piety. This is not goodness; this is goody-goodness. It is laughable.* It is a mockery of true religion.

Therefore, when you do some act of charity, practice some self-discipline, or pray, be on your guard! No self-publicity! Do not even publicize your good deeds to yourself. ("Do not let your left hand know what your right hand is doing.") Become inwardly detached from your goodness and do not care whether anyone should ever see all the sacrifices you have made for God or for other people.

Begin thinking this way: God, my Father, sees and knows what I have done. That is enough. I want no other reward except the reward He has in store for me.

---

*In this passage we have an example of Jesus' humor. He is smiling at the foolish hypocrites.

127

Appendix IV

"THIS IS HOW YOU SHOULD PRAY"
Suggestions on How to Pray, Based on the "Lord's Prayer"   (Matthew 6:9-13)

*"Our Father in heaven. . . ."**

Think of God as a loving, unseen, yet present Father, deeply aware and concerned in your needs, as well as the needs of your fellow disciples and those of the whole world. When you address God in prayer, say, "Father." This in itself is the first and greatest act of prayer, to turn from ourselves to the universe and say, "Father," "Our Father." (Compare Romans 8:15; Galatians 4:6.)

"Thy name be hallowed. . . ."

In prayer to God concentrate first of all on God Himself. Do not rush in with all your needs and wishes. He knows you and what you need before you ask Him, but you do not know Him. Quiet your heart and become aware of His greatness and goodness. Pray that you and all men might hallow His fatherly name, that is, worship Him.

"Thy kingdom come, thy will be done, on earth as in heaven."

As you come alive to His presence begin seeking His will. Again do not rush in with your will, with your desires and requests. It may be that in the moment you think you have something that you want God to do, He has something infinitely more important that He wants you to do. His will is so much greater than our will, so much wiser, so much more loving. His will takes in both your

New English Bible translation used throughout this study of the Lord's Prayer.

life and the life of the whole world. It is so much broader and stronger. It is by His will that the worlds were created. His will sustains history and only what He wills will finally survive. Learn to love His will, to seek it every day. Let the prayer, "Thy will be done," become the very core of your being. Around this prayer organize your life. Learn to quiet yourself again and again before the will of God.

"Give us today our daily bread. Forgive us the wrong we have done, as we have forgiven those who have wronged us. And do not bring us to the test, but save us from the evil one."

Now, having hallowed God's name, having opened yourself to His will, bring to Him your needs. Do this, not because God does not know your needs without your mentioning them, but simply because God delights in responding to you in a personal way. He loves you and wants to relate to you as a living personality, not as though you were some dumb animal. Your will, your faith, your love, and your initiative are important to Him. He wants to take them into account in His care of the world. So do not hesitate asking Him for your needs, so long as you honor Him and seek His will.

Appendix V

PROPERTY ATTITUDES CHECKLIST
Based on the Teaching of Jesus Found in Matthew 6:19-34

Put a check mark in the blank space in front of each statement after you are sure you understand it and can fully subscribe to it.

1.—— *I have firmly decided to take an unselfish and detached attitude toward my possessions and share them with those in need (6:19, 20).*

In order to carry out this decision in a faithful way:

2.—— I have undertaken an examination of my attitudes toward the things I *currently* possess to discover to what extent I consider them "mine" and therefore am personally bound up with them. On the basis of this self-examination I can say that my property is not my "treasure" (6:21).

3.—— I have also examined my attitude toward things I do not possess, to discover to what extent my life is darkened by the evil eye of covetousness. In the light of this I can also say I am free from the desire for other people's property (6:22, 23).

4.—— I have asked myself whether I am motivated by the quest for money rather than by the service of God's will, and I am settled in my heart that God rather than money has first place in my life (6:24).

5.—— *I have firmly decided to put away anxious thoughts about my physical needs* (6:25).
In order to carry out this decision in a faithful way:

6.—— I have sought to deepen my awareness of how much more meaning life has than simply food, clothing, or shelter (6:25).

7.—— I have considered how little control I have over my material existence and hence how futile it is to worry (6:27).

8.—— Most important, I have thought about the reality of God's love until I truly do believe that the "Father" knows what I need and will care for me in the same way He cares for the lesser parts of His creation (6:26, 28-32).

9.—— I have also come to understand the wisdom of the maxim: Each day has troubles enough of its own (6:34).

10.—— *In summary: I have decided to put first in my life God's kingdom and all that that entails by way of a just, loving, and righteous life with others, trusting that as I do so everything else necessary for my livelihood will be provided* (6:33).

Appendix VI

FOUR CONCLUDING ADMONITIONS
(Matthew 7:1-12)

The Sermon on the Mount comes to a close with four concluding admonitions in 7:1-12. These are followed by four closing warnings in the final section, 7:13-27.

The four admonitions, 7:1-12, look back on the teaching already given and answer the following questions:

1. How shall I use this teaching in relation to fellow disciples (7:1-5)?

2. How shall I use this teaching in relation to those outside the community of disciples (7:6)?

3. How can I ever attain to the life indicated by this teaching (7:7-11)?

4. How should I conduct myself in situations not covered by this teaching (7:12)?

Answer to Question 1:

Never take a condemning attitude toward anyone. Use this teaching first and foremost as a criticism of your own life. Only when you have dealt with your faults will you see clearly enough to help your brother overcome his.

Answer to Question 2:

In bringing this teaching to the world be alert to a type of person who mocks at truth. Do not carelessly press these "pearls" of the kingdom upon such men. It will only have bad consequences.

Answer to Question 3:

You can find power to live as Jesus taught through thoughtful (seeking), earnest (knocking) prayer, spurred on by the hope and the confidence that God is good and will give us every good thing we need.

Answer to Question 4:

In summary, let this be your guide in every situation: Consider how you would like others to treat you; then treat others that same way.

Appendix VII

FOUR CLOSING WARNINGS
A Summary Based on Matthew 7:13-27

1. Do not be discouraged by those *outside* the disciple community who seem to have it easy in comparison to yourself.

To win life in its fullest requires the kind of self-denial and discipline suggested by the Sermon on the Mount. Those who drift along with the crowd following every whim and desire will end up in disaster. Life belongs to those who "strive" to enter the narrow door of moral and spiritual transformation (Matthew 7:13, 14; compare Luke 13:23).

Neither be misled by those *inside* the Christian community who appear to be disciples, but do not practice what Jesus taught (7:15-27).

In particular:

2. Beware of *perverse prophetic personalities*, powerful leaders who "dress up" like disciples, but underneath are full of greed, turning the blind trust of the "sheep" to their own gain. The best way to recognize this destructive type is by paying careful attention to the results of their work. Are the fruits good or bad, in conformity to the teaching of Jesus or against it? (7:15-20)

3. Beware of *lawless miracle workers,* proud of their ability to preach Christian sermons and perform miraculous deeds, proud of their piety but careless about "doing" the will of God. Remember,

pious words and spectacular wonderworkings are not enough to gain entrance into the kingdom of God. "Wicked ways" spoil everything else (7:21-23).

4. Beware of *foolish men,* ordinary Christians who try to get along without acting on what Jesus taught. Like men who build a house on surface soil without bothering to dig down to bedrock (compare Luke 6:47-49), their lives lack solid foundation (7:24-27).

Only those who lay a foundation below the surface on the hard rock of obedience to the "words" of Jesus will survive the flood tides and judgments of time and eternity.

BIBLIOGRAPHICAL COMMENTS

1. A very helpful textual commentary on the Sermon on the Mount is now available in a revised paperback edition: A. M. Hunter, *A Pattern for Life, An Exposition of the Sermon on the Mount,* The Westminster Press, 1965. For a simple down-to-earth exposition of the Sermon on the Mount in terms any teenager can understand, see Clarence Jordan's booklet, *The Sermon on the Mount,* Judson Press, 1952. There is also much food for thought in Dietrich Bonhoeffer's *The Cost of Discipleship,* SCM Press, 1959. This spiritual classic is based for the most part on Matthew 5 to 7.

2. Those who might be interested in knowing more about the suggestion that the Sermon on the Mount functioned in the early church as a catechism, as well as the approach of contemporary biblical scholarship to this section of the New Testament, should consult Joachim Jeremias, *The Sermon on the Mount,* Fortress Press, 1963, as well as W. D. Davies, *The Sermon on the Mount,* Cambridge University Press, 1966.